THE

10

Most Important
Things You
Can Say to a

MASON

RON RHODES

HARVEST HOUSE PUBLISHERS
Eugene, Oregon 97402

Cover by Terry Dugan Design, Minneapolis, Minnesota

The 10 Most Important Things Series
by Ron Rhodes

The 10 Most Important Things You Can Say to a Catholic
The 10 Most Important Things You Can Say to a Jehovah's Witness
The 10 Most Important Things You Can Say to a Mason
The 10 Most Important Things You Can Say to a Mormon

Also by Ron Rhodes
Angels Among Us
The Complete Book of Bible Answers
Find It Fast in the Bible
Miracles Around Us
Reasoning from the Scriptures with Catholics
Reasoning from the Scriptures with Masons
Reasoning from the Scriptures with the Jehovah's Witnesses
Reasoning from the Scriptures with the Mormons
What Did Jesus Mean?

THE 10 MOST IMPORTANT THINGS YOU CAN SAY TO A MASON

Copyright © 2002 Ron Rhodes
Published by Harvest House Publishers
Eugene, Oregon 97402

Library of Congress Cataloging-in-Publication Data
Rhodes, Ron.
  The 10 most important things you can say to a Mason / Ron Rhodes.
    p. cm. — (The 10 most important things series)
  Includes bibliographical references (p.).
  ISBN 0-7369-0536-7
    1. Freemasonry—Religious aspects—Christianity. I. Title: Ten most important things you can say to a Mason. II. Title.
HS495.R53 2002
366'.1—dc21   2001038504

Printed in the United States of America.

02   03   04   05   06   07   / BP-CF /   10   9   8   7   6   5   4   3   2   1

This book is dedicated to the countless Christians across America who hold full-time jobs (often more than 40 hours per week), have families to take care of at home, and are very busy in life's various endeavors—yet still desire to become equipped to defend the truth of Christianity against errant teachings. May this little book assist you in reaching that worthy goal!

Acknowledgments

A special thanks to the staff at Harvest House Publishers for coming up with the idea for this concise book about witnessing to Masons. All of us agree there is a need for such a resource.

I also want to take this opportunity to thank those who contacted me following the publication of my earlier book, *Reasoning from the Scriptures with Masons* (a considerably longer book—supplementary to the present volume—which is available in Christian bookstores). Your words of encouragement and your commitment to the cause of apologetics among errant groups have been an inspiration to me.

Most of all, as always, I give a heartfelt thanks to my wife, Kerri, and my two children, David and Kylie, without whose support it would truly be impossible for me to do what I do.

Contents

Ten Critical Points

This book is short by design. The chapters *in* this book are short by design. I believe there is much to be said for brevity. However—and I want to emphasize this very strongly—*brevity should not be thought of as "shallowness."* This book contains ten critical points to share with your Mason friends, but the points are concise and succinct. This book is intended to provide you with the most important apologetic information in the briefest possible fashion. In a day of information overload, the merits of such an approach seem obvious.

I devote an entire chapter to each of the ten most important points you can make to a Mason. Each chapter presents one primary point, and there are a number of supportive arguments in each chapter that substantiate that particular point. My desire is that you would become thoroughly equipped to lead the Mason to the true God, the true Jesus, and the true gospel of grace of which the New Testament speaks. I pray that God will use you to bring Masons out of the kingdom of darkness and into the kingdom of light—the kingdom of Jesus Christ (see Colossians 1:13,14).

Of course, I realize there are some Masons who claim to be Christians already. In the case of the "Christian" Mason, the first goal is to make sure the person *is* a Christian according to the biblical definition. A secondary goal is to provide substantive reasons why the "Christian" Mason should no longer be affiliated with the Masonic Lodge.

Whether you are dealing with a Christian or non-Christian Mason, it could be that the concise information in this book will cause you to want to go deeper and learn even more about interacting with Masons of all sorts. That is a good thing. The more you learn, the more God can use you in witnessing. In such a case, I urge you to dig into my larger volume *Reasoning from the Scriptures with Masons,* which is significantly more comprehensive than the book you are holding in your hands. You will find that these two books complement each other. For your convenience, at the end of each of the following chapters I provide relevant page numbers from *Reasoning from the Scriptures with Masons.*

Icons Used in this Book

To make this guide easy to follow and understand, the icons below are used to highlight specific sections in each chapter.

 The Masonic Lodge's position on a particular doctrine.

 Key points to remember regarding the Masonic position.

 The biblical position on a particular doctrine.

 An important point when refuting a Masonic belief or supporting biblical truth.

 A closer look at an important word, verse, or historical insight.

 A witnessing tip.

 Proceed with caution on a particular point.

 Quick-review checklist of apologetic points.

 Digging deeper—recommends supplementary reading from my book *Reasoning from the Scriptures with Masons*.

If you run into witnessing trouble, feel free to contact Reasoning from the Scriptures Ministries. We will help you if we can.

Ron Rhodes
Reasoning from the Scriptures Ministries
P.O. Box 80087
Rancho Santa Margarita, CA 92688

www.ronrhodes.org

Free newsletter available upon request.

1

Masonry

Is Not Just a Fraternal Organization—It Is a Religion

 One of the more controversial aspects of Freemasonry is the question of whether or not it is a religion. Even Masons disagree among themselves on this issue.

Well-known Masonic authors Henry Wilson Coil and Albert Pike say Freemasonry *is* a religion. They say Freemasonry requires a belief in a Supreme Being and actively involves temples, doctrines, altars, worship, and even chaplains. Such factors indicate Freemasonry is a religious organization.

Coil asserted that "Freemasonry is undoubtedly a religion,"[1] and compared the Masonic Lodge to a church.[2] Masonry "is a religion without a creed, being of no sect but finding truth in all."[3] "The fact that Freemasonry is a mild religion does not mean that it is no religion."[4] He argued that "Freemasonry certainly requires a belief in the existence of, and man's dependence upon, a Supreme Being to which he is responsible. What can a church add to that, except to bring into fellowship those who have like feelings? That is exactly what the Lodge does."[5] He suggested that "only by judging from external appearances and applying arbitrary gauges can we say that Freemasonry is not religion."[6]

Albert Pike likewise said that "every Masonic Lodge is a temple of religion, and its teachings are instruction in religion."[7] He argued that "the ministers of this religion are all Masons who comprehend it and are devoted to it; its sacrifices to God are good works."[8] He believed Masonry "is the universal, eternal, immutable religion, such as God planted it in the heart of universal humanity."[9] He alluded to James 1:27 in defense of his position: "Religion that God our Father accepts as pure and faultless is this: to look after orphans and widows in their distress and to keep oneself from being polluted by the world." Thus, Masonry is a *works-oriented* religion.

There are other Masons who, while not explicitly calling Masonry a "religion," nevertheless make statements that imply Masonry is "religious" or is a "religious institution." Albert Mackey makes this claim in his *Encyclopedia of Freemasonry.*[10]

The Altar: A Sacred Utensil

The altar "is a sacred utensil of religion, intended, like the altars of the ancient temples, for religious uses, and thus identifying Masonry, by its necessary existence in our Lodges, as a religious institution. Its presence should also lead the contemplative Mason to view the ceremonies in which it is employed with solemn reverence, as being part of a really religious worship."[11]

Other Masons—the majority, in fact—deny that Freemasonry is a religion. They acknowledge that it requires belief in a Supreme Deity and the immortality of the soul. But they say the differences between Freemasonry and religion are far greater than any similarities that may exist. They point out that the term "religion" implies new revelation, a plan of salvation, a theology, dogmas, sacraments, clergy, and ways of communicating with God. Freemasonry has none of these things, it is claimed.[12] Freemasonry is said to be "religious," but not a religion. Alphonse Cerza writes, "Freemasonry cannot be a religion because it has no creed; it has no confession of faith; it has no theology, no ritual of worship."[13] Freemasonry is viewed not as a religion, but as a philosophy. "Freemasonry is a philosophy or system of morals and ethics based on the commonly held beliefs of all monotheistic religions. It therefore cannot, and does not, tell any man how to find the will of God, because it is not religion."[14]

Because each Mason is free to interpret religious ideas as he chooses, many argue from this as well that Freemasonry cannot be categorized as a religion. How the individual Mason perceives and worships the Supreme Being is his own business, as is the means by which he hopes to attain immortality, and no brother Mason is permitted to attempt to dissuade him from those beliefs.

In Freemasonry, then, a person is free to follow his own personal religious beliefs—whether he is a Christian, a Jew, a Muslim, or a Hindu. "He may believe the teachings of any organized religion, or he may even have religious convictions that are his alone—as did Thomas Jefferson and John Locke—so long as he believes in a Supreme Being. On that basis, Masonry has welcomed Jews, Moslems, Sikhs, and others, all of whom take the oaths on their own Holy Books."[15] Masonry thus brings together people of different persuasions to enjoy a common fellowship, despite different personal religious beliefs.[16]

These Masons believe Freemasonry is more about ethics and doing good in the world than about religion.[17] "Instead of teaching men what to believe, men are simply asked to put the religion they already have, when they become a Mason, into everyday practice."[18] Freemasonry "teaches Masons that their daily life should reflect the principles of their own religion, whatever *their religion* might be."[19]

It is fair to say that, despite the controversy over this issue, *most* Masons today believe Freemasonry is *not* a religion. One likely reason for this is that it would be hard for Masonry to draw people into its ranks from a variety of religious persuasions if it positioned itself as a new religion.

 Beware that not all Masons are consistent in their statements regarding whether Masonry is a religion. One of the most highly respected Masons of times past, Albert Pike, made contradictory statements on the issue. Whereas Pike in one place declared that "every Masonic Lodge is a temple of religion, and its teachings are instruction in religion,"[20] in another place he said, "Masonry is not a religion. He who makes of it a religious belief, falsifies and denaturalizes it."[21]

Masonry as a Religion: The Masonic View

- Some Masons say Freemasonry is a religion in view of the fact that it requires belief in a Supreme Being and involves temples, doctrines, altars, and worship.

- Other Masons—the majority—say Freemasonry is not a religion, but is rather a system of ethics based on the commonly held beliefs of all monotheistic religions.

 The evidence supports the view that Freemasonry is a religion. 1) Masonry requires belief in a deity and even teaches a concept of God; 2) Masonry involves typical religious furniture and ceremonies; 3) Masonry fits dictionary and encyclopedia definitions of religion; 4) the claim that Masonry is just "religious" but not a "religion" is a hollow one; 5) Masonry is a religion that finds truth in all religions; and 6) many Christian denominations and other religious organizations have taken a stand against Masonry because of its religious teachings.

 Masonry requires belief in a deity and even teaches a concept of God. Masonic author Joseph Fort Newton asserted that "everything in Masonry has reference to God, implies God, speaks of God, points and leads to God. Not a degree, not a symbol, not an obligation, not a lecture, not a charge but finds its meaning and derives its beauty from God the Great Architect, in whose temple all Masons are workmen."[22] Mason Martin Wagner likewise said, "It is to him [God] that Masonic altars are built, priests consecrated, sacrifices made, temples erected and solemnly dedicated."[23]

God is *worshiped* within Masonic Lodges, which is something that clearly marks the Masonic Lodge as a religious institution. Mason Carl Claudy tells us that "Freemasonry's Lodges are erected to God....Symbolically, to 'erect to God' means to construct something in honor, in worship, in reverence to and for him. Hardly is the initiate within the West Gate before he is impressed that Freemasonry worships God."[24]

 Masonry involves typical religious furniture and ceremonies. Within Masonic Lodges one will find altars, pulpits, "Worshipful Masters," rituals, prayers, pledges, sacred vows, reading from sacred literature, the singing of hymns, and funeral services. The presence of such things constitutes a strong argument that Freemasonry is a religion. Regarding the importance of the altar, Albert Mackey said that "the most important article of furniture in a Lodge room is undoubtedly the altar....It is an altar of sacrifice, for on it the candidate is directed to lay his passions and vices as an oblation to the Deity, while he offers up the thoughts of a pure heart as a fitting incense to the Grand Architect of the Universe. The altar is, therefore, the most holy place in a Lodge."[25] If one argues that, despite the presence of the altar and other religious elements, Freemasonry is *not* a religion, one could by that same virtue argue that Christianity is not a religion.

 Masonry fits dictionary and encyclopedia definitions of religion. Webster's Third *New International Dictionary* defines religion as involving "a personal awareness or conviction of the existence of a supreme being or of supernatural powers or influences controlling one's own, common humanity's, or all nature's destiny."[26] The *Encyclopedia Britannica* defines religion as "consisting of a person's relation to God or to gods or spirits. Worship is probably the most basic element of religion, but moral conduct, right belief, and participation in religious institutions are generally also constituent elements of the religious life as practiced by believers and worshipers."[27]

 Ask your Mason friend to consider:

- Does Freemasonry advocate a personal awareness or conviction of the existence of a Supreme Being? *(Yes.)*

- Does Freemasonry focus attention on a person's relation to God? *(Yes.)*

- Does worship take place within Masonic Lodges? *(Yes.)*

- Does Freemasonry emphasize moral conduct? *(Yes.)*

- Does Freemasonry involve participation in a religious institution? *(Yes.)*

In view of such factors, a good case can be made that Freemasonry is a religion, since authoritative encyclopedias and dictionaries define "religion" according to these factors.

The claim that Masonry is just "religious" but not a "religion" is a hollow one. This claim has yielded considerable discussion among both Masons and critics of Masonry. The important point is that using an *adjective* instead of a *noun* doesn't really change anything. In fact, Masonic authority Henry Wilson Coil pointed out that "to call Masonry not religion but religious merely substitutes an adjective for a noun, both meaning the same thing. It is as absurd as saying that a certain individual has no intellect but is intellectual, or that he has no wealth but is wealthy."[28] Christian apologists John Ankerberg and John Weldon add that it would be just as ridiculous as saying a man has no power but is powerful, or he has no courage but is courageous, or he has no patience but is patient, or that he has no honor but is honorable.[29]

 Ask your Mason friend: Can a person have no intellect but be intellectual? Can a person have no power but be powerful? Can a person have no courage, yet be courageous? Likewise, does it make sense to say the Masonic Lodge is not a religion but is religious?

 Masonry is a religion that finds truth in all religions. Many Masons argue that, because Freemasonry is open to all religions, this means that it is *not* a religion. However, such thinking is fallacious. Hinduism also believes that all paths lead to God, yet this tolerance on the part of Hinduism does not negate the fact that it is a religion.[30] Just as Hinduism is a religion despite the fact that it acknowledges the truth of many religions, so Freemasonry is a religion that sees truth in many religions.

Mason Manly Hall, in apparent agreement with this assessment, affirmed that the true Mason "realizes with the divine illumination of his lodge that as a Mason his religion must be universal: Christ, Buddha, or Mohammed, the name means little, for he recognizes only the light and not the bearer. He worships at every shrine, bows before every altar, whether in temple, mosque or cathedral, realizing with his truer understanding the oneness of all spiritual truth."[31]

 Ask your Mason friend: Did you know that Hinduism is classified as a religion, even though it believes that all religious paths lead to God? Did you know that the Baha'i faith is a religion, even though it embraces all religions within its fold? In view of these facts, can you see why a good case can be made that Freemasonry is a religion, even though it sees truth in many religions?

 Many Christian denominations and other religious organizations have taken a stand against Masonry because of its religious teachings. These include the Roman Catholic Church, the Eastern Orthodox Church of Greece, the Lutheran Church Missouri Synod, the Reformed Presbyterian Church, the Church of God, the Orthodox Presbyterian Church, the Pentecostal Church, the Church of the Nazarene, the Wesleyan Church, the Mennonite Church, Seventh-day Adventists, and the Quakers. All these, in both Europe and America, have forbidden their members to join a Masonic Lodge.[32]

These churches take exception to common Masonic teachings such as the claim that all religions are true, that Christ is not truly God, that Christ is not the only way of salvation, and that the Bible is merely one among many "symbols" of religious truth. They see as untrue the Masonic teaching that all people of all religions are part of a single brotherhood. Scripturally, one does not become a part of the family of God without believing in the one true Savior, Jesus Christ (John 3:16; Acts 16:31; Titus 2:13,14).

Remind your Mason friend that the Masonic Lodge is an institution that

- claims to draw people closer to God
- claims to give people a clearer picture of their responsibility to God
- teaches the immortality of the soul
- asserts that entrance into the Celestial Lodge Above depends on following its moral dictates
- engages in worship
- makes use of rituals, prayers, and altars (with Bibles on them)
- calls the Lodge leader "Worshipful Master"

Such factors provide good reason to categorize Masonry as a religion.

Masonry Is Not Just a Fraternal Organization—It Is a Religion

- ✓ Masonry requires belief in a deity and even teaches a concept of God.
- ✓ Masonry involves typical religious furniture and ceremonies.
- ✓ Masonry fits dictionary and encyclopedia definitions of religion.
- ✓ The claim that Masonry is just "religious" but not a "religion" is a hollow one.
- ✓ Masonry is a religion that finds truth in all religions.
- ✓ Many Christian denominations and other religious organizations have taken a stand against Masonry because of its religious teachings.

For further information on the Masonic view of Masonry as a religion, I invite you to consult my book *Reasoning from the Scriptures with Masons,* pages 75–85.

Masonry

Does Not
Have Origins
in Biblical Times

 The origin of Freemasonry has been shrouded (some-times deliberately) in deep mystery and wild legends.
Some Masons have suggested that Masonic light is alluded to in the creation account: "In the beginning God created the heavens and the earth. Now the earth was formless and empty, darkness was over the surface of the deep, and the Spirit of God was hovering over the waters. And God said, *'Let there be light,' and there was light*" (Genesis 1:1-3, emphasis added). According to this theory, Masonry has existed from the very beginning.

Other Masons claim that Freemasonry goes back to the time of Adam and Eve, sometime after the creation. These point to Genesis 3:7 where we read that, following Adam and Eve's sin, "the eyes of both of them were opened, and they knew that they were naked; and they sewed fig leaves together and made themselves loin coverings." We are told that the fig leaves were the first Masonic "aprons."[1] In Freemasonry such aprons are used in various initiatory rituals.

One of the more popular theories, held by many Masons, is that Freemasonry dates back to the time of Solomon, who made use of the skills of stonemasons when erecting the temple in Jerusalem (see 1 Kings 5 and 2 Chronicles 2:3-16).[2] It is argued that Hiram, the King of Tyre, aided Solomon in the building of the Jerusalem Temple by supplying trees, carpenters, and masons, and that Solomon was the Grand Master of the Masonic Lodge at Jerusalem.[3]

Other Masons claim that Masonry ultimately finds its origin in the ancient pagan religions that existed in biblical times. John Robinson documents the fact that claims have been made "to establish the origins of Masonry in ancient Egypt, and some traced Masonic sources to the Essenes, Zoroastrians, Chaldeans, and especially the Phoenicians."[4]

Still other Masonic historians have claimed Masonic membership for such luminaries as Abraham, Noah, Moses, Ptolemy, Julius Caesar, and Pythagoras.[5] Such claims are rarely made with evidence or substantiation, and Masons who make such claims should be challenged to provide ironclad proof for their allegations.

Masonic Origins: The Masonic View

- Some Masons argue that Masonry is alluded to in the creation account.

- Others suggest Masonry began during the time of Adam and Eve.

- Many Masons believe that Masonry began with Solomon.

- Still others hold that Masonry is rooted in the pagan religions of biblical days.

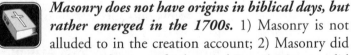

Masonry does not have origins in biblical days, but rather emerged in the 1700s. 1) Masonry is not alluded to in the creation account; 2) Masonry did not emerge during the time of Adam and Eve; 3) Masonry did not emerge during the time of Solomon; 4) Masonry does not derive from the ancient pagan mystery religions; and 5) Historically, Masonry emerged in the early 1700s.

 Masonry is not alluded to in the creation account. In his book *Scottish Rite Masonry Illustrated,* J. Blanchard claims:

> When the spirit of God moved upon the face of the waters; when the great Jehovah ordained the creation of the world; when the first Sun rose to greet with its beams the new morning and the august command was uttered: "Let there be light;" the lips of deity breathed Masonry into existence and it must live forever; for truth is eternal, and the principles of truth are the foundation of Masonry.[6]

Such words are nothing more than eisogesis. (*Eisogesis* refers to reading a meaning *into a text,* such as the text of Scripture. The proper method is *exegesis,* which refers to deriving the meaning *from* the text.) There is virtually nothing in Genesis or the rest of Scripture to warrant the idea that Genesis 1:1-3 refers to God's creation of Masonic light. The context indicates that the creation of *physical* light is described in Genesis 1, for we are told that "God called the light 'day,' and the darkness he called 'night'" (verse 5).

 Masonry contradicts Bible doctrine at numerous points. It is therefore impossible that the "light" of the Bible and the "light" of Freemasonry come from the same source (God). For example, Masonry typically views Jesus as just a good moral teacher, whereas the Bible views Him as God. Masonry says salvation hinges on ethical living, whereas the Bible says it is based entirely on faith in Christ. Help your Mason friend understand how biblical "light" and Masonic light differ.

 Masonry did not emerge during the time of Adam and Eve. Masonic rituals are nowhere to be found in the context of Genesis 3, not to mention the rest of the Bible. (This is another example of Masons practicing eisogesis instead of exegesis.) The fig leaves in Genesis 3 had the sole purpose of covering Adam and Eve's nakedness; they were not used in any rituals or initiatory ceremonies. (It is highly telling that a number of recent Masons have acknowledged their embarrassment over this far-fetched Adam-and-Eve theory.)

 Ask your Mason friend to read aloud from Genesis 3:1-7 and then show you specifically where there is any allusion to Masonic rituals or a fraternal organization.

 Masonry did not emerge during the time of Solomon. Masons often argue that Solomon made use of the skills of stonemasons when erecting the temple in Jerusalem (see 1 Kings 5 and 2 Chronicles 2:3-16), and that Hiram, the King of Tyre, aided Solomon in the building of the Jerusalem Temple by supplying trees, carpenters, and masons. Solomon himself was the Grand Master of the Masonic Lodge at Jerusalem.

It is true that Scripture speaks of King Hiram providing materials to Solomon for the building of the temple. It is also true that Hiram provided Solomon with expert workmen. But there is no mention in Scripture of Freemasonry, nor is there any mention in Scripture of a fraternal organization made up of Masons. There is certainly no mention of Hiram and Solomon being bound by any kind of Masonic ties.[7]

Consider the biblical facts about Hiram and his relationship with Solomon. Read through 1 Kings 5 below, and as you do so, contemplate whether you think this account depicts 1) a king assisting another king in a building project, or 2) the beginnings of the Masonic Lodge.

> When Hiram king of Tyre heard that Solomon had been anointed king to succeed his father David, he sent his envoys to Solomon, because he had always been on friendly terms with David. Solomon sent back this message to Hiram:

>> You know that because of the wars waged against my father David from all sides, he could not build a temple for the Name of the LORD his God until the LORD put his enemies under his feet. But now the LORD my God has given me rest on every side, and there is no adversary or disaster. I intend, therefore, to build a temple for the Name of the LORD my God, as the LORD told my father David, when he said, "Your son whom I will put on the throne in your place will build the temple for my Name."

>> So give orders that cedars of Lebanon be cut for me. My men will work with yours, and I will pay you for your men whatever wages you set. You know that we have no one so skilled in felling timber as the Sidonians.

> When Hiram heard Solomon's message, he was greatly pleased and said, "Praise be to the LORD today, for he has given David a wise son to rule over this great nation."

> So Hiram sent word to Solomon:

>> I have received the message you sent me and will do all you want in providing the cedar and pine logs. My men will haul them down from Lebanon to the sea, and I will float them in rafts by sea to the place you specify. There I will separate them and you can take them away. And you are to grant my wish by providing food for my royal household.

> In this way Hiram kept Solomon supplied with all the cedar and pine logs he wanted, and Solomon gave Hiram

twenty thousand cors of wheat as food for his household, in addition to twenty thousand baths of pressed olive oil. Solomon continued to do this for Hiram year after year. The LORD gave Solomon wisdom, just as he had promised him. There were peaceful relations between Hiram and Solomon, and the two of them made a treaty.

King Solomon conscripted laborers from all Israel—thirty thousand men. He sent them off to Lebanon in shifts of ten thousand a month, so that they spent one month in Lebanon and two months at home. Adoniram was in charge of the forced labor. Solomon had seventy thousand carriers and eighty thousand stonecutters in the hills, as well as thirty-three hundred foremen who supervised the project and directed the workmen. At the king's command they removed from the quarry large blocks of quality stone to provide a foundation of dressed stone for the temple. The craftsmen of Solomon and Hiram and the men of Gebal cut and prepared the timber and stone for the building of the temple.

 After reading through 1 Kings 5, ask your Mason friend: What is your assessment? Is this passage referring to one king helping another king? Or does it portray the origins of Freemasonry? (The truth is, there is not even a hint of any kind of fraternal organization in this passage.)

One reason the narrative about Solomon's temple is so important to Masons is that much of their modern ritual is based upon it. Modern Masons often refer to Solomon's temple as the most perfect edifice ever erected by man. It has come to symbolize, in an allegorical fashion, the perfect development of mind in character and virtue.[8] In other words, just as the ancient stonemasons sought perfection in the building of the physical temple of Solomon, so Masons today seek perfection in the building of character and virtue in their own lives. To be sure, character and virtue are good things, but trying to find Masonic origins in Solomon is an exercise in futility.

 Masonry does not derive from the ancient pagan mystery religions. Though it is true that some of the rituals of Masonry have strong parallels to some of the ancient mystery religions, it is not true that there is an unbroken line of development between these ancient religions and modern Masonry. Those who suggest such an idea are revising Masonic history to suit themselves. Freemasonry may have *borrowed* some of its ritual from the ancient mystery religions, but Freemasonry did not *derive* from them. (We will look at the relationship of Masonry to the mystery religions in chapter 8.)

The truth is that many of the claims for the origin of Freemasonry are nothing more than fanciful. According to critic John Robinson, "All of the various theories of the origins of Freemasonry are legendary. Not one of them is supported by any universally accepted evidence."[9]

Profound Uncertainty

"Freemasonry is itself profoundly uncertain of its own origins. In the four centuries or so of its formal existence, it has endeavored, sometimes desperately, to establish a pedigree. Masonic writers have filled numerous books with efforts to chronicle the history of their craft. Some of these efforts have been not just spurious, but, on occasion, positively comical in their extravagance, naïveté and wishful thinking."[10]

 Historically, Masonry emerged in the early 1700s. Documented history reveals that Freemasonry *formally* began in London, England, in A.D. 1717, through the efforts of Anglican clergymen James Anderson, George Payne, and John Theophilus Desaguliers.[11] This was when the Grand Lodge of London was first organized. Prior to this time, there was no Grand Lodge, and there were no Grand Masters to lead the Grand Lodge.

As apologist Robert Morey notes, what was founded in 1717 involved "Speculative Masonry," which is distinct from "Operative Masonry." Here is the backdrop: During the Middle Ages and after, there were "Operative Masons," so called because they worked in the construction trades as builders, stonemasons, and architects.[12] They were *working* masons engaged in the construction of great churches and cathedrals in Europe.

And "as with any other trade during the Middle Ages, there was a guild of stone masons who traveled from one building site to another."[13] James Rongstad tells us that "because they usually worked closely together and because they frequently were away from home, they formed a tight-knit group in which they shared discussions on philosophies, politics, religion, and all other interests of their society."[14] Forming a guild not only served to protect them but also served to enhance their professional credibility.[15]

As to why these operative Masons were called "*Free*masons," a number of possibilities have been suggested by researchers. Some believe that because these men worked with "free stone" that could be easily carved, they became known as "free stone masons"—later shortened to "Freemasons."[16] Others believe they were called Freemasons because they were free to move around from city to city, or country to country.[17] Others say that perhaps these were just free men as opposed to serfs, and still others say that as traveling workmen they were given freedom in the towns in which they worked.[18] My personal feeling is that the second option above is correct—that is, they were "Freemasons" because they were free to move around from city to city, or country to country, while engaging in their profession.

There is no evidence that at this early juncture the guild of "Freemasons" had secret rituals and ceremonies, degrees, and a vast array of symbols derived from the Bible and other religions.[19] It was more or less a professional union.

The Grand Lodge that was founded in London in 1717 was not part of this "Operative Masonry" (involving professional builders) that had existed for quite some time, but rather was engaged in "Speculative Masonry" (involving nonbuilding masons). Membership in Masonic Lodges today is *totally* speculative.[20] Speculative masonry is "another name for Freemasonry in its modern acceptance."[21]

While the old operative Masons were engaged in building cathedrals and temples, which were dedicated to the service and worship of God, Albert Mackey tells us that "the Speculative Mason is engaged in the construction of a spiritual temple in his heart, pure and spotless, fit for the dwelling place of Him who is the author of purity; where God is to be worshiped in spirit and in truth, and whence every evil thought and unruly passion are to be banished."[22] Hence, we see that the *old* work of the stonemasons is allegorically applied today in a *new* way to the building of a pure and undefiled heart. Many of the symbols that are used in Masonic Lodges are actually tools that stonemasons would use in construction, but they are allegorically interpreted to refer to the development of some particular virtue in the life of the modern Mason. Later in the book I will address how the Masonic view of salvation hinges on ethics and the building of virtue in the heart.

Masonry Does Not Have Origins in Biblical Times

✓ Masonry is not alluded to in the creation account, nor did it emerge during the time of Adam and Eve or the time of Solomon.

✓ Masonry does not derive from the ancient pagan mystery religions.

✓ Historically, Masonry—more specifically, Speculative Masonry—emerged in the early 1700s.

 For further information on Masonic origins, consult *Reasoning from the Scriptures with Masons,* pages 9 and 31–42.

Masonic Rituals

Are Highly
Offensive

Following the opening of a Lodge meeting, the formal business commences. Part of that business relates to new candidates seeking to join. The candidate is not considered unless he is a worthy individual who has been vouched for by another Mason in good standing. The candidate's petition is reviewed, as are his character and reputation, and a vote is taken in the Lodge. A single negative vote, as evidenced by a "black ball," is enough to bar the candidate's petition.[1] But if no black ball appears, the candidate is declared duly elected.[2]

The Masonic Candidate

"A candidate for Freemasonry must be a man of good reputation and integrity and well fitted to become a member of the lodge in which he seeks initiation."—*Freemason's Guide and Compendium*, p. 259

The new member promptly goes through the ritual for the Entered Apprentice degree, a ritual which would impress most people as quite bizarre. One researcher summarizes it this way:

> The typical ceremony begins with the initiate being first divested of his jacket and his tie and any money or metal articles he has. His left trouser leg is then rolled up over the knee, his shirt is opened to expose his left breast, and his right shoe is removed and replaced by a slipper. Then the person who is to be initiated will have a blindfold put on him and a noose put around his neck. This is called a "Cable Tow." The blindfolded initiate *(they call this being "hoodwinked")* is brought, with the noose around his neck, to the outer door of the Lodge.
>
> The candidate thus attired is said to be in darkness, an allegory of Masonry that signifies that everyone outside of Masonry is in darkness and that only Masons have the true knowledge that will bring light to the world.
>
> The new Mason is brought to the outer door seeking the light of the Lodge, and there the Doorkeeper, or Tiler, will put a sword or a sharp point to his breast and lead him into the lodge room, where an altar sits in its center. The lodge members await the candidate in the darkness that surrounds the altar, which is lit from a single light above. Behind the altar stands a man called "The Worshipful Master." He is the master of the Lodge and presides over the initiation.
>
> When the initiate is brought before him, he bows before "The Worshipful Master" and says something like this: "I am lost in darkness, and I am seeking the light of Freemasonry." He is then told he is entering into a secret organization and that he must keep the secrets he is going to be taught.
>
> At this time he is required to take a blood initiation oath. Every Mason who joins the Lodge takes his thumb or his

hand to his throat and repeats an oath that has been
repeated by every Mason who has joined the Lodge.[3]

Swearing a blood oath is required not just for the Entered
Apprentice degree, but for the other degrees of Freemasonry as
well. Before a candidate takes such oaths, however, the Master
assures him that the oath will not interfere with any duty that
is owed to God, country, family, or friends.[4]

After expressing his willingness to take the oath, the candidate, still blindfolded, is led into the proper position for an
Entered Apprentice. He kneels on his bare left knee, with his
right leg in front of him in the angle of a square. Before him on
the altar is the opened holy book of his faith (the Bible for Christians, the Koran for Muslims, and the Vedas for Hindus), with
the compass and square on the open book.[5] The candidate then
places his left hand under the book, palm up, while his right
hand is on top of the compass and square, palm downward,[6]
and utters an oath in which he promises not to reveal the secrets
of the Lodge to anyone. At one point in the oath, he says:

> All this I most solemnly, sincerely promise and swear, with
> a firm and steadfast resolution to perform the same,
> without any mental reservation or secret evasion of mind
> whatever, binding myself under no less penalty than that
> of having my throat cut across, my tongue torn out by its
> roots, and my body buried in the rough sands of the sea,
> at low-water mark, where the tide ebbs and flows twice in
> twenty-four hours, should I ever knowingly violate this
> my Entered Apprentice obligation. So help me God, and
> keep me steadfast in the due performance of the same.[7]

The oath for entrance into the Fellow Craft degree (the next
after the Entered Apprentice degree) includes these additional
words: "Binding myself under no less a penalty than that of
having my left breast torn open, my heart plucked out and given
as prey to the wild beasts of the fields and the fowls of the air."[8]

For those seeking entrance into the third degree—the Master Mason's degree—the oath adds:

> Binding myself under no less penalty than to have my body severed in twain and divided to the north and south, my bowels burnt to ashes in the center, and the ashes scattered before the four winds of heaven, that there might not the least track or trace of remembrance remain among men, or Masons, of so vile and perjured a wretch as I should be, were I ever to prove willfully guilty of violating any part of this my solemn oath and obligation of a Master Mason. So help me God, and keep me steadfast in the due performance of the same.[9]

Enough said!

The Entered Apprentice candidate, following his oath, is instructed to kiss the holy book as a token of his sincerity. He is then asked what he desires most, to which the proper answer is, "Light." At this response, the blindfold is promptly removed and the secrets of the Entered Apprentice are revealed to him. These include a secret handgrip and two hand signs.[10]

Following this, a lambskin (the "apron") is presented to the candidate. He is told that this white apron is an emblem of innocence "more ancient than the Golden Fleece or the Roman Eagle," more honorable a badge than any that could ever be bestowed by any prince or potentate.[11] The apron is an emblem of innocence that points to the purity of life necessary for one who seeks entrance into the Celestial Lodge Above (heaven).

There are some further elements contained in the Entered Apprentice ritual, but the above represents the heart of it.

Masonic Rituals: The Masonic View

- Freemasonry claims that the candidate is in darkness and Freemasonry can impart spiritual light to him. (Much of the ritual symbolizes this.)

- The candidate takes a blood oath, promising never to reveal to others the secrets of Freemasonry.

- The candidate is given a lambskin to symbolize the purity necessary to enter heaven.

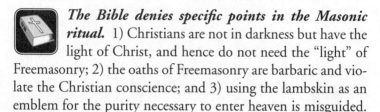

The Bible denies specific points in the Masonic ritual. 1) Christians are not in darkness but have the light of Christ, and hence do not need the "light" of Freemasonry; 2) the oaths of Freemasonry are barbaric and violate the Christian conscience; and 3) using the lambskin as an emblem for the purity necessary to enter heaven is misguided.

Christians are not in darkness but have the light of Christ, and hence do not need the "light" of Freemasonry. How can a Christian, in good conscience, bow before a "Worshipful Master" and say, "I am in darkness and I am in need of the light of Freemasonry"? After all, the Christian has received the light of the world (Jesus Christ) and has been redeemed by His blood. Through Christ, we have been delivered from the kingdom of darkness and brought into His kingdom—the kingdom of God's Son— which is the kingdom of light (Colossians 1:12-14). As God's children, we walk in the light, not in darkness (see 1 John 1:5-7). In John 12:46 Jesus said, "I have come into the world as a light, so that no one who believes in me should stay in darkness." He also said, "I am the light of the world. Whoever follows me will never walk in darkness, but will have the light of life." The apostle Paul affirmed this: "You were once darkness, but now you are light in the Lord. Live as children of light" (Ephesians 5:8). Christians have already escaped the defilement of the dark world system, and are enlightened by the Word of God (2 Peter 1:3,4; Psalm 119:105).

Masons sometimes cite 2 Corinthians 4:6 in support of the need for Masonic light.[12] This verse makes reference to "God, who said, 'Let light shine out of darkness.' " However, the verse quoted in its entirety shows that true light comes through Jesus Christ: "God, who said, 'Let light shine out of darkness,' made his light shine in our hearts to give us the light of the knowledge of the glory of God in the face of Christ." This verse tells us that the same God that illuminated the creation with physical light illuminates our hearts spiritually through Jesus Christ. As commentator Adam Clarke put it, "It is in and through Jesus that we can receive the divine light, and it is in and by him that we can be made partakers of the divine glory."[13]

If the Mason to whom you are talking claims to be a Christian, ask him how he can honestly say in the Masonic ritual, "I am lost in darkness, and I am seeking the light of Freemasonry." Ask him how he interprets John 8:12, John 12:46, Colossians 1:12-14, and Ephesians 5:8. Gently ask him if he has considered the possibility that his participation in the Masonic ritual represents a denial of his Christian faith.

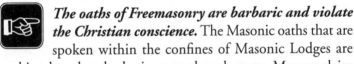

The oaths of Freemasonry are barbaric and violate the Christian conscience. The Masonic oaths that are spoken within the confines of Masonic Lodges are nothing less than barbaric, even though many Masons claim the oaths are not to be taken literally. One pro-Mason historian claims, "No Mason believes that the penalties of his oath will be visited upon him, and every candidate would hurry out of the room if ever told that he must help to inflict those penalties on someone else."[14] Still, the very spirit of such oaths is offensive to any moral conscience, let alone the conscience of a Christian.

In opposing such oaths, some well-meaning Christians have taken a stand against oaths altogether by appealing to the words of Jesus in Matthew 5:33-37:

Again, you have heard that it was said to the people long
ago, "Do not break your oath, but keep the oaths you
have made to the Lord." But I tell you, Do not swear at
all: either by heaven, for it is God's throne; or by the earth,
for it is his footstool; or by Jerusalem, for it is the city of
the Great King. And do not swear by your head, for you
cannot make even one hair white or black. Simply let your
"Yes" be "Yes," and your "No," "No"; anything beyond
this comes from the evil one.

The problem with citing this particular passage against the
Masonic use of oaths is that there are other verses in Scripture
which do, in fact, indicate that certain kinds of oaths are allow-
able. Aside from the legitimate oaths mentioned in the Old Testament (Leviticus 5:1; 19:12; Numbers 30:2-15; Deuteronomy
23:21-23), there are some mentioned in the New Testament as
well (Acts 2:30; Hebrews 6:16-18; 7:20-22). Even the apostle
Paul said, "I call God as my witness..." (2 Corinthians 1:23),
just as he also said, "I assure you before God that what I am
writing to you is no lie" (Galatians 1:20). From a biblical stand-
point, there are at least *some* cases in which oaths or oathlike
statements can be made.

What, then, are we to make of Jesus' words in Matthew 5:33-
37? The problem Jesus was dealing with in this passage is rooted
in Pharisaism. The Pharisees promoted the use of oaths to affirm
that someone was telling the truth, and the oath always involved
some type of curse that the person placed on himself if his word
was not true or the promise was not fulfilled. It got to the point
that one assumed someone was not telling the truth if an oath
was not attached to his statement.

Jesus was against *this* use of oaths. He was telling His followers that their character, their reputation for honesty, and the
words they spoke should be so consistently true, undefiled, and
without duplicity that no one would ever think it necessary to
put them under an oath. By constantly adding oaths to our

verbal statements, we are implying to others that our usual speech is untrustworthy. It should not be that way.

Having said all this, the real problem Christians have with Masonic oaths is not the fact that oaths are taken, but the *content* and *purpose* of those oaths. No Christian has any business taking oaths that speak of cutting his throat or tearing out his tongue if he gives away the secrets of the Lodge.

In my view, if a Christian joins a Masonic Lodge and participates in this bloody oath—and then later realizes the terrible mistake he has made—he is best off *breaking* his oath and leaving the Masonic Lodge. Better to break an "earthly" oath than to remain committed to one that is clearly wrong and against God's will (see Leviticus 5:4).

It is likely that many Christians who have taken the Masonic oaths have taken them under false pretenses. After all, before taking the oath, the candidate is assured that the oath will not interfere with any duty that is owed to God, country, family, or friends. This is flatly false, since the oath most certainly does interfere with one's duty to the one true God of the Bible. Walton Hannah, author of *Darkness Visible: A Christian Appraisal of Freemasonry,* makes this point forcefully:

> An oath taken on false pretenses is null and void. Suppose, to take an extreme and unlikely example, a man interested in social work swore an oath of loyalty and secrecy to an organization on the express understanding that its aims were to provide holiday homes for tired mothers. After he has taken this oath it is revealed to him that the real aim of the society is to drop an atom bomb on Buckingham Palace. His oath of loyalty to that organization is obviously not binding in conscience, because it was taken on false grounds, and he could not fulfill it without sin. But in this instance, as a loyal citizen, he may well feel that the secrecy, too, is not binding on him; that it is his duty to inform the police, that he would be guilty of a serious sin

of omission were he to fail to do so....Now the Masonic oaths are taken on the express understanding that they can in no way conflict with a man's social, moral, or religious duties....The majority of Masons who take them, even good Christian Masons, do not appear to be aware of any conflict....But should a Christian initiate come to realize that Masonry in regarding all gods as equal, or in offering prayers which deliberately exclude our Lord, or in proclaiming the name of God in terms of heathen deities as in the Royal Arch (things which were not disclosed to him on initiation) does violate his Christian principles, his oath ceases to be binding in conscience.[15]

 Help your Mason friend see that the Masonic oath *does* conflict with what he owes to God. In the Royal Arch degree, for example, God's true name is said to be *Jabulon*—a construct that joins the name Yahweh (the God of the Bible) to the names of two false gods, Baal and Osiris. (The Bible condemns false gods—see Exodus 20:4-6; Leviticus 19:4; 26:1; Deuteronomy 4:15-19; 2 Samuel 7:22.) Also, though the Bible says we are to pray in the name of Jesus (John 14:13,14; 15:16; 16:23,24), the Masonic ritual excludes the name of Jesus from all prayers. There is no question that the Masonic ritual conflicts with our position before God.

Many Masons argue that the words in the Masonic oaths are only to be understood symbolically. Jim Tresner, for example, writes: "Some anti-Masonic writers have complained about the so-called 'penalties' in the Masonic obligations. Those penalties are purely symbolic and refer to the pain, despair, and horror which any honest man should feel at the thought that he had violated his sworn word."[16]

However, as Christian apologists John Ankerberg and John Weldon have noted, "No candidate entering into Masonry is told during the ritual that the penalties of the oaths he is swearing to are merely symbolic. In his mind, there is no reason for him not to believe that every Masonic obligation deals with vows of literal life and death."[17] Either the oaths mean what they say or they do not. If the oaths *do* mean what they say, then the Mason is entering into a bloody pact consenting to his own murder by barbarous torture and mutilation as a penalty for violation. If the oaths *do not* mean what they say, then the person is swearing, with his hands on a Bible, something that is absolutely not taken seriously. This gravely abuses the holy Bible.[18]

 Ask your Mason friend: If the Masonic oaths *do* mean what they say, does this mean you are entering into a pact consenting to your own murder as a penalty for violation? But if the oaths *do not* mean what they say, are you swearing with your hands on a Bible something that is not taken seriously? How do you then interpret the Masonic stipulation that the oaths are to be taken "without any mental reservation or secret evasion of mind whatever"?

Some Masons try to lighten the barbarism of the oaths by saying it is never Masons who are responsible for inflicting the penalties of the oaths, but rather only God: "No Mason swears to inflict the penalties, but only invites them down on his own head. There has never been any indication whatsoever of just what person or power is supposed to carry out the penalty, and since the oath is taken on the Holy Bible it is highly likely that God was being asked to take on that responsibility."[19]

 The cutting of throats is a *human* technique of execution, not a *divine* technique. Do Masons expect us to believe that God would reach down from heaven with a physical hand and knife and slit someone's throat? Ask your Mason friend about this.

***Using lambskin as an emblem for the purity neces-
sary for entrance into heaven is misguided.*** Masons
often cite biblical passages in support of their view that
the lambskin is an emblem of the purity necessary to gain
entrance into the Celestial Lodge Above. For example, in
Exodus 12:3-5 the Israelites are instructed to use a lamb that is
"without defect" in their sacrifices. In Isaiah 53:7-9 we find a
prophecy of the Lamb of God, who is blameless and spotless. In
John 1:29, John the Baptist makes reference to Jesus as the Lamb
of God, who is without sin. In 1 Peter 1:19, we find reference
to a "lamb without blemish or defect." Then in Revelation 5:8-
13, we find reference to the Lamb of God in heaven, who is
portrayed as holy. In view of such verses, Masons say "the lamb
has in all ages been deemed an emblem of innocence." [20]

It is eternally true that the Lamb of God (Jesus) is sinless,
spotless, and without defect of any kind. It is also true that
God's people in Old Testament times were called to use lambs
that were without defect in their sacrifices. But the Masonic
adaptation of these verses that argues for a lambskin as an
emblem of the personal purity necessary for entrance into
heaven is completely at odds with the Bible. Let us consider
Revelation 5:8-13 as an example:

> The four living creatures and the twenty-four elders fell
> down before the Lamb. Each one had a harp and they
> were holding golden bowls full of incense, which are the
> prayers of the saints. And they sang a new song: "You are
> worthy to take the scroll and to open its seals, because
> you were slain, and with your blood you purchased men
> for God from every tribe and language and people and
> nation. You have made them to be a kingdom and priests
> to serve our God, and they will reign on the earth."
>
> Then I looked and heard the voice of many angels, num-
> bering thousands upon thousands, and ten thousand times
> ten thousand. They encircled the throne and the living

creatures and the elders. In a loud voice they sang: "Worthy is the Lamb, who was slain, to receive power and wealth and wisdom and strength and honor and glory and praise!"

Then I heard every creature in heaven and on earth and under the earth and on the sea, and all that is in them, singing: "To him who sits on the throne and to the Lamb be praise and honor and glory and power, for ever and ever!"

Consider this passage in terms of the broader teachings of the book of Revelation. Notice that the "Lamb" (Christ) in the book of Revelation is the one slain for our salvation (Revelation 5:6). He alone is found "worthy" (5:12) and is worshiped (5:8). Any victory the saints have is *through His merits* (12:11), not because of our works. Thus we are *His* followers and sing *His* praises. We do not earn salvation by the personal purity represented by the Masonic lambskin. Rather, the salvation of believers hinges entirely on the fact that Christ, as the Lamb of God, *purchased* our salvation at Calvary.

 The Bible is emphatic that "it is by grace you have been saved, through faith—and this not from yourselves, it is the gift of God—not by works, so that no one can boast" (Ephesians 2:8,9). "He saved us, not because of righteous things we had done, but because of his mercy" (Titus 3:5). "To the man who does not work but trusts God who justifies the wicked, his faith is credited as righteousness" (Romans 4:5). In view of such verses, the Masonic teaching about salvation by human effort, as represented by the lambskin, is unbiblical. Share these verses with your Mason friend.

 Masons point to the phrase "a lamb without blemish or defect" in 1 Peter 1:18,19 as a support for the emblem of the lambskin, which represents the purity of life necessary to enter heaven. However, the *entire* passage reads this way: "You know that it was not with perishable things such as silver or gold that you were redeemed from the empty way of life handed down to you from your forefathers, but with the precious blood of Christ, a lamb without blemish or defect." This verse centers on salvation in *Jesus alone*. If Masons take this verse seriously, they should accept it for what it really says: Christ is the *only* means of salvation because He is the Lamb of God who laid down His life on behalf of sinners.

As the Lamb of God, Jesus affirmed that it was for the very purpose of dying that He came into the world (John 12:27). He declared that His death was a sacrificial offering for the sins of humanity (Matthew 26:26-28). He took His sacrificial mission with utmost seriousness, for He knew that without Him, humanity would certainly perish (Matthew 16:25) and spend eternity apart from God in a place of great suffering (Luke 16:22-28). Help your Mason friend see that the personal purity that yields entrance into heaven comes only through being cleansed by the blood of Jesus, shed on his behalf (1 John 1:7).

Masonic Rituals Are Highly Offensive

✓ Christians are not in darkness but have the light of Christ, and hence do not need the "light" of Freemasonry.

✓ The oaths of Freemasonry are barbaric and violate the Christian conscience.

✓ Using the lambskin as an emblem for the purity necessary for entrance into heaven is misguided.

For further information on the Masonic rituals, consult *Reasoning from the Scriptures with Masons*, pages 53–73.

4

The Bible

Is Not Just One of Many Holy Books—It Is Uniquely God's Word

 Masons believe that even though the Bible is a significant book, it is not the exclusive Word of God. As one Mason put it, "Masonry as such refuses to distinguish, or to confine the divine revelation exclusively to, the tenets or writings of any one particular faith, realizing that all contain elements of vital truth."[1]

Masons often refer to the Bible as a symbol of God's will. "The prevailing Masonic opinion is that the Bible is only a symbol of Divine Will, Law, or Revelation, and not that its contents are Divine Law, inspired, or revealed. So far, no responsible authority has held that a Freemason must believe the Bible or any part of it."[2] Other symbols of God's will include the Koran (used by Muslims), the Vedas (used by Hindus), and the Pentateuch (used by Jews).

All holy books are acceptable within the confines of any Masonic Lodge. To the Mason, all these books provide not just religious truth but *moral* truth and hence constitute ethical guides by which to govern one's life. This is the important thing for the Mason.[3]

Many Masons take an esoteric approach to the Bible. This is an approach that seeks hidden meanings in its pages. Albert Pike believed the biblical books "were written in symbols unintelligible to the profane" (that is, to the ignorant).[4] Richard Thorn likewise said that "Jesus taught in parables...to impart hidden knowledge to a select few; not for capricious reasons, but because the larger group was not yet prepared to hear and understand."[5]

Thorn's words are a clear allusion to Jesus' words to the disciples in Matthew 13, where we're told that "the disciples came to him and asked, 'Why do you speak to the people in parables?'" Jesus answered, "The knowledge of the secrets of the kingdom of heaven has been given to you, but not to them" (Matthew 13:10,11). Hence, Thorn says, apparently even Jesus endorsed an esoteric approach to the Bible.

Only for the Worthy

Masonry "conceals its secrets from all except the Adepts and Sages, or the Elect, and uses false explanations and misinterpretations of its symbols to mislead those who deserve only to be misled....Truth is not for those who are unworthy or unable to receive it, or would pervert it."—Albert Pike

The Bible: The Masonic View

- The Bible is not exclusively the Word of God.
- Other holy books include the Hindu Vedas and the Muslim Koran.
- The important thing about these books is that they teach ethical guidelines by which to live.
- The Bible is generally interpreted esoterically.

The Bible is not one of many holy books, but is rather the unique Word of God. 1) The Bible contradicts other "holy books" on essential doctrines; 2) God says that His revelation in the Bible should not be added to; 3) the Bible is inspired; 4) the Bible is as authoritative as God Himself is; 5) archaeology supports the veracity of the Bible; and 6) an esoteric approach to interpreting the Bible is unreliable.

 The Bible contradicts other "holy books" on essential doctrines. This means that if the Bible is correct, the other books are necessarily *in*correct, since these books set forth ideas on basic religious concepts that are diametrically opposed to the Bible. Furthermore, these books do not agree among themselves.

Consider the doctrine of God, which is the most fundamental doctrine of any religious system. According to the Christian Bible, Jesus taught that there is one personal God who is triune in nature (Mark 12:29; John 4:24; 5:18,19). Muhammad (the prophet of Islam) taught in the Koran that there is only one God, but that God cannot have a son. In fact, the Koran teaches that the very idea that God can have a son is blasphemous. Confucius in his writings was polytheistic *(there are many gods)*. The words of Krishna represent a combination of polytheism and pantheism *(all is god)*. Zoroaster in his writings set forth religious dualism *(there is both a good god and a bad god)*. Buddha taught that the concept of God was essentially irrelevant. Clearly, the leaders of the world's major religions, as indicated in their "holy books," held completely contradictory views regarding the nature of God. And since the doctrine of God is the most fundamental doctrine of any religious system, it cannot legitimately be said that all these "holy books" are true.

There are other significant differences. The Koran and Vedas, for example, set forth a works-oriented view of salvation, whereas the Bible says salvation is a free gift for those who trust in Christ alone (Ephesians 2:8,9). While Hinduism and Buddhism teach reincarnation, Christianity denies this and teaches that we live once, die once, and then face the judgment (Hebrews 9:27). While Christianity teaches that Jesus is absolute deity, the Baha'i faith calls Him a mere manifestation of God, and Islam calls Him just a prophet of God (who is lesser than Muhammad). Muslims say Jesus did not die on the cross, for it would have been unthinkable for Allah to have allowed one of his prophets to be crucified. But Christianity teaches that Jesus died for our sins (Matthew 20:28). Muslims view the Bible as being corrupted (Suras 2:75; 2:78,79), whereas Christians believe it is inspired by God (2 Timothy 3:16,17) and has been accurately copied through the centuries.

We see, then, that there are many irreconcilable points of difference between the Bible, the Vedas, the Koran, and other "holy books" such that if one is right, the others *must* be wrong. If the Bible *is* God's Word, then the others *cannot* be God's Word.

 Ask your Mason friend:

- Did you know that, while Jesus taught a triune concept of God (Matthew 28:19), the Muslim Koran denies the Trinity and says God cannot have a son?

- Did you know that, while the Muslim Koran and the Hindu Vedas set forth a works-oriented view of salvation, the Bible teaches salvation is a free gift by faith in Christ?

- Did you know that, while Hinduism teaches reincarnation, the Bible teaches we live once, die once, and then face judgment (Hebrews 9:27)?

- In view of such irreconcilable differences, wouldn't you agree that if one of these holy books is truly right, the others must necessarily be wrong?

God says that His revelation in the Bible should not be added to. Solomon warned that "every word of God is tested....Do not add to His words or He will reprove you, and you will be proved a liar" (Proverbs 30:5,6 NASB). The apostle John closed the last part of the Bible with the same exhortation, declaring, "I warn everyone who hears the words of the prophecy of this book: If anyone adds to them, God will add to him the plagues described in this book. And if anyone takes words away from this book of prophecy, God will take away from him his share in the tree of life" (Revelation 22:18,19). God obviously does not wish anything that claims divine authority to be added to His inspired words. Those who set forth other holy books, books that in reality are man-made documents, fall under God's condemnation.

Even if one hypothetically granted that God did wish to reveal additional truths through other holy books (which I do not grant), that revelation would have to be consistent with previous divine revelation. The apostle Paul said that "even if we or an angel from heaven should preach a gospel other than the one we preached to you, let him be eternally condemned!" (Galatians 1:8). Paul spoke of the importance of ensuring that new claims to truth be measured against what we *know* to be true from known Scripture (see Acts 17:11; 2 Timothy 3:16). Since the "revelations" in the Hindu Vedas and the Muslim Koran and other such books directly contradict the revelation found in the pages of the Christian Bible, we can assume they did not come from the same source. If the Bible came from God, then these other books *did not.*

 Share with your Mason friend that God does not contradict Himself. With that fundamental principle in mind, point out that, since the "revelations" in the Hindu Vedas and the Muslim Koran contradict the Bible on *numerous* doctrines (such as the nature of God, the identity of Jesus, and the requirement for salvation), it is logical to assume that these "revelations" did not come from the same source. Don't let him sidestep this important issue.

 The Bible is inspired. The Christian Bible is unique because it is *inspired*. Inspiration doesn't mean the biblical writer just felt enthusiastic, like the writer of the "Star-Spangled Banner." Nor does it mean the writings are necessarily inspiring to read, like an uplifting poem. The biblical Greek word for *inspired* literally means "God-breathed." Because Scripture is breathed out by God—because it *originates* from Him—it is true and inerrant.

Biblical inspiration may be defined as God's superintending of the human authors so that, using their own individual personalities—and even their writing styles—they composed and recorded *without error* His revelation to humankind in the words of the original manuscripts. In other words, the original documents of the Bible were written by men who, though permitted to exercise their own personalities and literary talents, wrote under the control and guidance of the Holy Spirit, the result being a perfect and errorless record of the exact message God desired to give to humankind.

Second Peter 1:21 provides a key insight regarding the human-divine interchange in the process of inspiration. This verse informs us that "prophecy [or Scripture] never had its origin in the will of man, but men spoke from God as they were carried along by the Holy Spirit." The phrase *carried along* in this verse literally means "forcefully borne along."

Even though human beings were used in the process of writing down God's Word, they were all "borne along" by the Holy Spirit. The human wills of the authors were not the originators of God's message. God did not permit the will of sinful human beings to misdirect or erroneously record His message. Rather, "God *moved* and the prophet *mouthed* these truths; God *revealed* and man *recorded* His word."[6]

The Greek word for "carried along" in 2 Peter 1:21 is the same as that found in Acts 27:15-17. In this account, experienced sailors could not steer their vessel because the wind was so strong. The ship was being *driven, directed,* and *carried along* by the wind. This is similar to the Spirit's driving, directing, and carrying along the human authors of the Bible as He wished. Yet, just as the sailors were active on the ship (though the wind, not the sailors, controlled the ship's movement), so the human authors were active in writing as the Spirit directed. Help your Mason friend understand that the Bible is not a mere human book.

In 2 Timothy 3:16 we read, "All Scripture is God-breathed and is useful for teaching, rebuking, correcting and training in righteousness." The Greek form of "God-breathed" (or "inspired") in this verse is passive. This means the Bible is the *result* of the "breath of God." The origin of the Bible—both Old and New Testaments—is thus seen to be God.

In view of this, it is obvious that the Bible is not just one among many other so-called "holy books," as Masons claim. The Bible is truly inspired and is derived from God. And because the Bible is inspired (unlike the Muslim Koran and Hindu Vedas), it alone speaks with the authority of God.

 The Bible is as authoritative as God Himself is. Scripture alone is the supreme and infallible authority for the believer (2 Peter 1:21; 2 Timothy 3:16,17; 1 Corinthians 2:13). Jesus and the apostles often gave testimony to the absolute authority of the Bible. Jesus affirmed the Bible's divine inspiration (Matthew 22:43), its indestructibility (Matthew 5:17,18), infallibility (John 10:35), final authority (Matthew 4:4,7,10), historicity (Matthew 12:40; 24:37), scientific accuracy (Matthew 19:3-5), and factual inerrancy (John 17:17; Matthew 22:29).

Scripture has final authority because it is a direct revelation from God, and carries the very authority of God Himself (Galatians 1:12). For this reason, Jesus said, "Scripture cannot be broken" (John 10:35). He declared, "I tell you the truth, until heaven and earth disappear, not the smallest letter, not the least stroke of a pen, will by any means disappear from the Law until everything is accomplished" (Matthew 5:18). He asserted, "It is easier for heaven and earth to disappear than for the least stroke of a pen to drop out of the Law" (Luke 16:17). Jesus used Scripture as the final court of appeal in every matter under dispute. To the Sadducees He said, "You are in error because you do not know the Scriptures or the power of God" (Matthew 22:29). To the devil, Jesus consistently responded, "It is written..." (Matthew 4:4-10). Following Jesus' lead, we must conclude that Scripture alone is our supreme and final authority.

 Archaeology supports the veracity of the Bible. Unlike other books that claim to be Scripture, the Bible's accuracy and reliability has been verified over and over again by archaeological evidence found by both believing *and* nonbelieving scholars and scientists. This evidence includes verification of numerous customs, places, names, and events mentioned in the Bible.

For instance, it was formerly claimed that Moses couldn't have written the first five books of the Bible because handwriting hadn't yet been invented at that time. But archaeological finds now conclusively demonstrate that there indeed was handwriting during the time of Moses, and hence the claims of critics have been silenced.

Addressing how archaeology has continually verified the reliability of the Bible, scholar Donald J. Wiseman notes, "The geography of Bible lands and visible remains of antiquity were gradually recorded until today more than 25,000 sites within this region and dating to Old Testament times, in their broadest sense, have been located."[7] Well-known scholar William F. Albright, following a comprehensive study, wrote: "Discovery after discovery has established the accuracy of innumerable details, and has brought increased recognition of the value of the Bible as a source of history."[8]

An esoteric approach to interpreting the Bible is unreliable. The Masonic appeal to Matthew 13:10,11 in support of an esoteric approach to the Bible is not valid. In this passage, Jesus is reported as being in front of a mixed multitude comprised of both believers and unbelievers. He did not attempt to separate the believers from the unbelievers and then instruct only the believers. Rather, He constructed His teaching so that believers would understand what He said but unbelievers *would not*—and He did this by using parables.

After Jesus had taught using one such parable, a disciple asked Him, "Why do you speak to the people in parables?" (Matthew 13:10). Jesus answered: "The knowledge of *the secrets* of the kingdom of heaven has been given to you [believers], but not to them [unbelievers]" (verse 11, emphasis added). Masons conclude that, in view of this verse, there must be secrets in the words of Jesus that only true "believers" can discern.

However, the Greek word for *secret* in this passage simply means "mystery." A mystery in the biblical sense is a truth that cannot be discerned simply by human investigation, but requires special revelation from God. Generally, this word refers to a truth that was unknown to people living in Old Testament times, but is now revealed to humankind by God (Matthew 13:17; Colossians 1:26). In Matthew 13, Jesus provides information to believers about the kingdom of heaven that has never been revealed before.

One might legitimately ask why Jesus engineered His teaching in parables, so that believers could understand His teaching but unbelievers could not. The backdrop is that the disciples, having responded favorably to Jesus' teaching and having placed their faith in Him, already knew much truth about Him as the Messiah. Careful reflection on Jesus' parables would enlighten them further. However, hardened unbelievers who had persistently refused Jesus' previous teachings were prevented from understanding the parables. Jesus was apparently following an injunction He had given earlier, in Matthew 7:6 in the Sermon on the Mount: "Do not give dogs what is sacred; do not throw your pearls to pigs." (Yet there is grace even here. It is possible that Jesus may have prevented unbelievers from understanding the parables because He did not want to burden them with more responsibility by imparting new truth for which they would be held accountable.)

One should not miss the fact that the parables of the sower (Matthew 13:3-9) and the tares (13:24-30) show that Jesus wanted His parables to be clear to those who were receptive. Jesus Himself provided the interpretation of these parables for His disciples. He did this not only so there would be no uncertainty as to their meaning, but to guide believers in the proper interpretation of the other parables. The fact that Christ did not interpret His subsequent parables shows that He fully expected believers to understand what He taught through following the method He had illustrated for them. Clearly, then, Matthew 13 does not support but rather argues *against* an esoteric method of interpreting Scripture.

Right from the first book in the Bible, there is virtually no indication that Scripture was intended to be taken esoterically. Rather, a plain (nonesoteric) reading of the text seems to be assumed throughout. A plain reading of Genesis indicates that when God created Adam in His own rational image, He gave Adam the gift of intelligible speech, thus enabling him to communicate objectively with his Creator (and with other human beings) via sharable linguistic symbols called words (Genesis

1:26). Indeed, God sovereignly chose to use human language as a medium of revelational communication.

If God's primary purpose for originating language was to make it possible for Him to communicate with human beings, as well as to enable human beings to communicate with each other, then it must follow that He would generally use language and expect man to use it in its literal, normal, and plain sense. This view of language is a prerequisite to understanding not only God's spoken word but His written Word (Scripture) as well.

 Masons may object and say that their interpretation of Scripture is as legitimate as anyone else's. Certainly everyone is entitled to his or her own interpretation of the Bible. At the same time, we must insist that not all interpretations are equally correct.

As Bible scholar Douglas Groothuis put it,

> Your interpretation is either true or false; you are either right or wrong. Having "your own interpretation" about the Bible does not, in itself, legitimate that interpretation as truth any more than "your interpretation" of your IRS return legitimates itself before the penetrating eyes of an income-tax auditor. He goes by "the book," not your book. The it's-my-interpretation cop-out may land you a big fine or even time behind bars (which no amount of creative interpretation will dissolve).[9]

 Jesus said His words lead to eternal life (John 6:63). But for us to receive eternal life through His words, they must be taken as He intended them to be taken. An esoteric reinterpretation of Scripture that yields *another Jesus* and *another gospel* (2 Corinthians 11:3,4; Galatians 1:6-9) will yield only eternal *death*. But eternal *life* comes from accepting the *real Jesus'* invitation:

"Whoever hears my word and believes him who sent me has eternal life and will not be condemned; he has crossed over from death to life" (John 5:24).

The Bible Is Not Just One of Many Holy Books—It Is Uniquely God's Word

✓ The Bible contradicts other "holy books" on essential doctrines.

✓ God says that His revelation in the Bible should not be added to.

✓ The Bible is inspired, and is just as authoritative as God Himself is.

✓ Archaeology supports the veracity of the Bible.

✓ An esoteric approach to interpreting the Bible is unreliable.

For further information on the Masonic view of the Bible, consult *Reasoning from the Scriptures with Masons*, pages 87–104.

The World Religions

Do Not All Worship the Same God

 God is described by Masons as the "Great Architect of the Universe," "Supreme Being," "Grand Geometrician of the Universe," "Grand Artificer of the Universe," and "God, the Creator, Author, and Architect of the Universe, Omnipotent, Omniscient, and Omnipresent."[1] Reading Masonic literature, one is given the distinct impression that the Supreme Being of the Masonic Lodge is essentially *unknowable* and, consequently, *inoffensive*. If God is infinitely beyond our ability to comprehend, then that means it is inappropriate for mere humans to fight over how to define Him.

In keeping with this, many Masons speak of God in general without addressing His individual attributes. William Hammond, for example, writes that Masonry "makes no attempt to explain how such a being came to be, nor to enumerate and define His divine attributes. It leaves its members free to their private views."[2]

The one key exception to Masons' avoidance of discussing God's attributes is their idea of God as the "all-seeing eye." According to Albert Mackey, the all-seeing eye "is a symbol of the omnipresent deity."[3] It is the same symbol, Mackey said,

God Undefined

"Freemasonry nowhere offers a definition of the nature and attributes of God, but leaves such matters to each individual to fashion as best he can. It asks of a man only that he believe that God is."—H. L. Haywood, *Great Teachings of Masonry*

that the Egyptians used to represent Osiris, their chief deity, in all their temples.[4] Mackey believed this all-seeing eye was alluded to in Proverbs 15:3, which tells us that "the eyes of the LORD are everywhere, keeping watch on the wicked and the good." The Psalms are also sometimes cited in this regard: "The eyes of the LORD are on the righteous and his ears are attentive to their cry" (Psalm 34:15); "indeed, he who watches over Israel will neither slumber nor sleep" (Psalm 121:4).

Masons believe that Jews, Christians, Hindus, Muslims, and those of other faiths are all worshiping the same "all-seeing" God but are using different names. God is "the nameless one of a hundred names."[5] As Mackey put it, "God is equally present with the pious Hindoo *[sic]* in the temple, the Jew in the synagogue, the Mohammedan in the mosque, and the Christian in the church."[6]

That said, however, Freemasonry *as an institution* refuses to affirm the Christian belief in God as a Trinity. Masons hold that, if Freemasonry were to affirm belief in the Trinity, this would amount to sponsoring the Christian religion, since Christianity is the only religion that holds to this doctrine. Rather, the Masonic policy is that "no phrase or terms should be used in a Masonic service that would arouse sectarian feelings or wound the religious sensibilities of any Freemason."[7]

One cannot help but see that, even though Freemasonry teaches that one is free to hold to one's own view of God, Masonry does in fact teach a concept of God—that is, that *all religions believe in the same God*. So, despite the fact that

Masonry denies teaching a doctrine of God, it does in fact teach such a doctrine. This is most evident in the Royal Arch degree of the York Rite, in which the Mason is told that the real name of God is *Jabulon*. This is said to be a compound word derived from "Ja" (for Jehovah), joined with "Bel" or "Bul" (for Baal, the ancient Canaanite God), and "On" (for Osiris, the ancient Egyptian mystery god).[8] We are told that "in this compound name an attempt is made to show by a coordination of divine names...the unity, identity and harmony of the Hebrew, Assyrian and Egyptian god-ideas, and the harmony of the Royal Arch religion with these ancient religions."[9]

God: The Masonic View

- God is the "Great Architect of the Universe," and is essentially unknowable.
- God's nature and attributes are generally left undefined.
- Members of different religions worship the same God using different names.
- The doctrine of the Trinity is avoided.
- The real name of God is "Jabulon"—derived from Jehovah, Baal, and Osiris.

The only true God is the God of the Bible. Scripture reveals that 1) the world religions are not worshiping the same God with different names; 2) God is knowable; 3) God is not "Jabulon"; 4) we can understand much about God through His divine attributes; 5) God is a Trinity; and 6) Masons are guilty of idolatry.

The world religions are not worshiping the same God with different names. A look at what the various religions teach about God proves the falseness of this notion. Since the Bible teaches the Trinity, the Muslim Koran *denies* the Trinity and exalts Allah, and the Hindu Vedas espouse millions of gods, the teaching of Freemasonry that the different religions are worshiping the same God using different names is founded in ignorance.

 If Yahweh is the one true God, as the Bible teaches (Exodus 3:14,15), then the god of Islam and the gods of Hinduism must be false gods. Help your Mason friend understand why this logically must be the case.

As an illustration, let us consider the Hindu view of God in more detail. While Christianity espouses a God that is eternally distinct from His creation, Hinduism is polytheistic, espousing belief in millions of gods. The Upanishads (one of the Hindu sacred Scriptures) teach that behind these many gods of Hinduism stands the one monistic ("all is one") reality of Brahman.[10] "Every aspect of the universe, both animate and inanimate, shares the same essentially divine nature. There is actually only one Self in the universe."[11]

According to this school of thought, every person possesses an individual soul known as *atman* that is related to the universal soul *(Brahman).*[12] All things in the universe (including humans) are viewed as extended from the being of Brahman. Our essence is said to be identical to that of Brahman.[13]

Because Hinduism sees all reality as "one," distinctions are considered unreal. When we perceive distinctions, it is nothing more than a mental illusion *(maya).*[14] "A person's individuality apart from the Brahman—the world in which one lives, that which one sees, hears, touches, and feels—is all an illusion, a dream."[15] As scholar Mark Albrecht put it, "Hinduism holds that the world is really 'Brahman in disguise'—all matter, especially biological and human life, is merely a temporary, illusory manifestation of this universal spirit."[16]

The big problem for humans, according to Hinduism, is that they are ignorant of their divine nature. People have forgotten they are extended from Brahman. When true knowledge of the illusion of life is fully realized (through many cycles of reincarnation), one can be freed from the bondage of life and achieve ultimate unity with Brahman.

In view of the above, isn't it obvious that Christians and Hindus are not worshiping the same God, and cannot—indeed, *must not*—worship together under one roof? If the Christian view of God is correct, then the Hindu view of God is necessarily *in*correct since it contradicts the Christian view at many points.

We can make this same point about the God of Islam. According to the Koran, Allah is the one true God. Allah is a unity; he can have no son. To say that God could have a son, Muslims say, is blasphemous—it implies some kind of sexual generation. Allah is *not* viewed as "the Father" (Suras 19:88-92; 112:3). He is viewed as transcendent, and seems more characterized by judgment, not grace; and by power, not mercy (Suras 6:142; 7:31).[17] By contrast, the Christian view is that God is a Trinity, that the first person of this Trinity is a "Father," that this Father has an eternal Son, that God is both transcendent *and* immanent, and that while God is characterized by judgment and power, He is also characterized by grace and mercy. The Christian view of God is incompatible with the Muslim view.

 Since both Hinduism and Islam hold to radically different ideas about God than does Christianity, isn't it clear that these religions are not espousing the same God at all? Isn't it fair to say that if the Christian view of God is correct, then the Hindu and Islamic views are *in*correct? Don't let your Mason friend sidestep this issue.

Scripture emphatically declares there is only *one* God. In Isaiah 44:8 God Himself asks, "Is there any God besides me? No, there is no other Rock; I know not one." In Isaiah 43:10, God declares: "Before me no god was formed, nor will there be one after me." That there is only one God is the consistent testimony of Scripture (John 5:44; 17:3; Romans 3:29,30; 16:27; 1 Corinthians 8:4; Galatians 3:20; Ephesians 4:6; 1 Thessalonians 1:9; 1 Timothy 1:17; 2:5; James 2:19; 1 John 5:20,21; Jude 25). This God is Yahweh (Exodus 3:14,15), not Allah and not the millions of gods of Hinduism.

 Some Masons may argue that the Bible says God is the Father of all human beings (and therefore *of all religions*) since He is their creator (Acts 17:24-28). Though it is true that Acts 17:28 indicates God is the divine "parent" of all creation, there is a more specific aspect of the fatherhood of God that relates *only* to those who become a part of His "forever family" by trusting in Christ. Help your Mason friend understand this important point.

John 1:12,13 tells us that "to all who received him *[Jesus]*, to those who believed in his name, he gave the right to become children of God—children born not of natural descent, nor of human decision or a husband's will, but born of God." Paul states in Galatians 3:26, "You are all sons of God through faith in Christ Jesus." Clearly, there is no universal fatherhood of God in the sense of everyone's being in His eternal family, for entrance into *this* family is restricted—it comes only by faith in Christ (see John 3:16; Acts 16:31).

Not only is God not everyone's "Father," some people actually have the *devil* as their "father." Jesus said to some Jews who wanted to kill Him, "You belong to your father, the devil, and you want to carry out your father's desire. He was a murderer from the beginning, not holding to the truth, for there is no truth in him. When he lies, he speaks his native language, for he is a liar and the father of lies" (John 8:44). John 8:47 indicates that if we do not do as God commands, we do not belong to Him. On a practical level, this means that if Masons do not do as God commands (such as trusting in Christ alone for salvation—John 3:16,17), they are not God's children and hence God is not their Father, as they claim. There is only one way into God's eternal family, and His name is Jesus Christ (see John 14:6; Acts 4:12; 1 Timothy 2:15).

 God is knowable. Contrary to the Masonry's implication that God is essentially unknowable, the Bible reveals that God is a personal being with whom deeply personal relationships can be established and enjoyed. A person is a conscious being—one who thinks, feels, and purposes, and carries these purposes into action. A person engages in active relationships with others. You can talk to a person, and get a response from him. You can share feelings and ideas with him. You can argue with him, love him, and even hate him if you so choose. Surely by this definition God must be understood as a person. After all, God is a conscious being who thinks, feels, and purposes—and He carries these purposes into action. He engages in relationships with others. You can talk to God and get a response from Him.

The biblical picture of God is that of a loving personal Father to whom believers may cry "Abba" (Romans 8:15). "Abba" is an Aramaic term of great intimacy, loosely meaning "daddy."

Jesus often spoke of God as a loving Father. Indeed, God is the "Father of compassion" of all believers (2 Corinthians 1:3). He is often portrayed in Scripture as compassionately responding to the personal requests of His people. (A few good examples may be found in Exodus 3:7,8; Job 34:28; Psalm 81:10; 91:14,15; 2 Corinthians 1:3,4; and Philippians 4:6,7.)

 Ask this of your Mason friend: Since God can be addressed by believers as "Abba" (daddy), and is the "Father of compassion," do you think the Masonic portrayal of God accurately reflects the biblical reality that we can enjoy an intimate, loving, personal relationship with Him? Which seems more appealing to you: the intimate God of the Bible or the distant Masonic deity? (Be ready to share verses such as Job

34:28; Psalms 81:10; 91:14,15; 2 Corinthians 1:3,4; and Philippians 4:6,7.)

 God is not "Jabulon." The Masonic claim that God's true name is *Jabulon* is atrocious, and the attempt to relate the God of the Bible to Baal is nothing less than blasphemy. Baal worship is the epitome of evil idol worship in the ancient world. It involved such things as ritual prostitution (Judges 2:17), self-mutilation (1 Kings 18:28), and the sacrificing (ritual murder) of little children (Jeremiah 19:4,5). In Judges 3:7 we read, "The Israelites did evil in the eyes of the LORD; they forgot the LORD their God and served the Baals and the Asherahs." From this, we can conclude that the Masonic view of God as "Jabulon" is detestable to the Lord.

The one sin for which God judged the people of Israel more severely than any other was that of participating in the false heathen religions (for example, Exodus 20:4-6; Leviticus 19:4; 26:1; Deuteronomy 4:15-19). The Bible repeatedly implies and states that God hates and utterly rejects anything associated with false religions and practices. Those who practice such idolatry are not seen as groping their way to God, but rather as having turned their backs on Him to follow the ways of darkness.

Not even all Masons are pleased with the idea of calling God "Jabulon." Albert Pike protested, "No man or body of men can make me accept as a sacred word, as a symbol of the infinite and eternal Godhead, a mongrel word, in part composed of the name of an accursed and beastly heathen God, whose name has been for more than 2000 years an appellation of the devil."[18] Though I disagree with most of what Pike believes, he is certainly right in this comment.

 Ask your Mason friend this: Did you know that in the Royal Arch degree, it is taught that God's true name is *Jabulon,* which is a compound word that blends the name *Jehovah* with the names of *Baal,* the ancient

Canaanite god, and *Osiris,* the ancient Egyptian mystery god? Were you aware that, according to the Bible, Baal worship was the epitome of evil idol worship in the ancient world—and involved such things as ritual prostitution (Judges 2:17), self-mutilation (1 Kings 18:28), and the sacrificing of little children (Jeremiah 19:4,5)?

 We can understand much about God through His divine attributes. Critic Walton Hannah says that in Freemasonry, "God is presented and titled in such terms that people of all reputable faiths may agree in a lowest-common-denominator deity shorn of all attributes distinctive of any single system of belief."[19] Contrary to Masonry, Scripture reveals that we can know a great deal about God—including some very specific attributes or perfections of God.

- *God is eternal.* God never came into being at a point in time. He is beyond time altogether. God is the King eternal (1 Timothy 1:17) who alone is immortal (6:16).

- *God is love.* God isn't just characterized by love—He is the very personification of love (1 John 4:8). Love permeates His being.

- *God is everywhere-present.* There is nowhere one can go where God is not (see Psalm 139:7,8; Jeremiah 23:23,24; Acts 17:27,28).

- *God is all-knowing.* God knows all things, both actual and possible (Matthew 11:21-23). He knows all things *past* (Isaiah 41:22), *present* (Hebrews 4:13), and *future* (Isaiah 46:10). Psalm 147:5 affirms that God's understanding "has no limit" (see also Psalm 139:11,12).

- *God is all-powerful.* He is *almighty* (Revelation 19:6), abundant in strength (Psalm 147:5), and has incomparably great power (2 Chronicles 20:6).

- *God is sovereign.* God rules the universe, controls all things, and is Lord over all (Ephesians 1). Nothing is beyond the reach of His control (see Psalms 50:1; 66:7; 93:1).

- *God is holy.* God's holiness means not just that He is entirely separate from all evil, but also that He is absolutely righteous (Leviticus 19:2). He is pure in every way (Psalm 71:22).

- *God is just.* God carries out His righteous standards justly and with equity. There is never any partiality or unfairness in God's dealings with people (Zephaniah 3:5; Romans 3:26).

These and many other attributes of God are revealed in the pages of the Bible, and show the falseness of the Masonic portrayal of God as essentially unknowable.

 God is a Trinity. To speak of God as *not* being a Trinity is to put forth a false view of God. C.S. Lewis once said that God Himself has revealed to us how we are to think of Him, and God Himself has revealed that He is a Trinity. Hence, for us to deny this doctrine or refuse to talk about it is to go against the way the one true God of Scripture has revealed Himself. Christians who attend a Masonic Lodge and go along with refusing to speak about the doctrine of the Trinity show their lack of commitment to the holy Scriptures.

Biblically, the doctrine of the Trinity is based on three lines of evidence: 1) there is only one true God (Isaiah 44:6,9; John 5:44; 17:3; Romans 3:29,30; 16:27; Galatians 3:20; Ephesians 4:6; 1 Timothy 2:5; James 2:19); 2) there are three persons who are God—the Father (1 Peter 1:2), the Son (John 20:28; Hebrews 1:8), and the Holy Spirit (Acts 5:3,4); and 3) there is three-in-oneness within the Godhead (2 Corinthians 13:14; Matthew 28:19).

Ask this question of your Mason friend: If God truly has revealed Himself to be a Trinity, is it not unwise to go along with the Masonic Lodge's policy of avoiding reference to God as a Trinity? How do you think God looks upon this?

Masons are guilty of idolatry. One scholar suggests that idolatry does not consist merely "in bodily kneeling before a material image; it consists in worshiping God under any other conception of him than that which is set before us in the gospels."[20] By this definition, Freemasonry is idolatrous.

The World Religions Do Not All Worship the Same God

- The world religions do not worship the same God with different names.
- God is knowable.
- God is not "Jabulon."
- We can understand much about God through His divine attributes.
- God is a Trinity.
- Masons are guilty of idolatry.

For further information on the Masonic view of God, consult *Reasoning from the Scriptures with Masons,* pages 105–30.

6

Jesus

Is Not Just a Good Moral Teacher—He Is Uniquely the Son of God

 The deity of Christ is either denied or greatly down-played within Masonic circles. Those who are Christians within the Masonic Lodge may consider Jesus to be the divine Son of God, but they typically choose not to invoke His name when praying, even if they believe He is divine.[1] Masons are instructed that "prayers in the lodges should be closed with expressions such as 'in the Most Holy and Precious name we pray,' using no additional words which would be in conflict with the religious beliefs of those present at meetings."[2]

If the name of Jesus were invoked during prayer, then others of different religious persuasions would seek to invoke the name of their deities during prayer. Since Masons seek to avoid religious disputes, invoking any name—including that of Jesus—is avoided. Prayers offered within the walls of the Masonic Lodge are universal in nature: "In its language citizens of every nation may converse; at its altars men of all religions may kneel; to its creed disciples of every faith may subscribe."[3] In keeping with this, Jesus' name is also stripped from Scripture quotations.

For the most part, Jesus is regarded by Masons more as a great moral teacher and ethical philosopher than as the divine

Avoidance of Jesus' Name

"The chaplain of the Masonic Lodge who prays as the voice of the lodge does not pray in the name of the Carpenter of Nazareth or the name of Jehovah or the name of Allah. He prays to the Grand Artificer or the Great Architect of the Universe. Under that title men of all faiths may find each his own deity."—Albert Pike, *Morals and Dogma*

Son of God. He is in the same league with other great men like Socrates.[4] He was a man who stood for virtue.

Some Masons go so far as to say that the reason Jesus was put to death was because of His high morality. Pike writes: "None can deny that [Jesus] taught and practiced a pure and elevated morality, even at the risk and to the ultimate loss of his life."[5] Although Jesus is admired, any suggestion that He is the only way to God is outright rejected by Masons. Such an idea is viewed as intolerant, and intolerance is not tolerated within the halls of Masonic Lodges. Masons believe there are many acceptable paths to God, all based on attaining a high level of morality.

According to some Masonic interpreters, Jesus taught that we are to be tolerant. Richard Thorn comments:

> Many people consider those of a different religion to be their enemies. Jesus said to love our enemies. Freemasonry teaches us to accept other people, and to respect their religious beliefs. It does not teach that all religions are equal, only that we should respect them. My religious concepts were formed long before I became a Mason, but I consider Freemasonry to be a work of the Lord Jesus Christ, raised up to emphasize that part of his teaching so often neglected by the church: to love your enemy.[6]

Jesus: The Masonic View

• The deity of Jesus is either denied or downplayed.

- Jesus' name is not invoked during prayers.
- Jesus' name is stripped from Scripture quotations.
- Jesus is viewed as a great moral teacher and ethical philosopher.
- Jesus' teachings on tolerance indicate we should be tolerant of other religions.

The Bible exalts Jesus as the divine Son of God. 1) Jesus was more than a good moral teacher; 2) Jesus is absolute deity; 3) Jesus' words about loving one another cannot be twisted to mean that we should ignore false doctrine; 4) Jesus' name should not be stripped from Bible references; 5) prayer should be in the name of Jesus; 6) Jesus died for our sins, not because of His high morality; 7) Jesus is the only way of salvation; and 8) the Jesus of Hinduism and the Jesus of Islam are radically different from the Jesus of the Bible, and hence Christians should not worship together with Hindus and Muslims.

Jesus was more than a good moral teacher. No mere "moral example" would ever claim that the destiny of the world lay in His hands, or that people would spend eternity in heaven or hell depending on whether they believed in Him (John 6:26-40). The only example this would provide would be one of mental imbalance. And for Jesus to convince people that He was God (John 8:58) and the Savior of the world (Luke 19:10) when He really was not would be the ultimate *im*morality:

> A man who was merely a man and said the sort of things Jesus said would not be a great moral teacher. He would either be a lunatic—on the level with the man who says he is a poached egg—or else he would be the Devil of Hell. You must make your choice. Either this man was, and is, the son of God: or else a madman or something worse (C.S. Lewis).[7]

Think about it. Would a person who was merely a good, moral teacher, and nothing more, tell people they would spend eternity in heaven or hell depending on whether they believed in him? Ask your Mason friend to give serious consideration to this issue.

Jesus is absolute deity. Masons often speak of God as being the Great Architect of the Universe, one of His names being Jehovah or Yahweh. But what they fail to recognize is the biblical teaching that *Jesus* is Yahweh.

A comparison of the Old and New Testaments provides powerful testimony to Jesus' identity as Yahweh. In Zechariah 12:10, for example, Yahweh is speaking prophetically: "They will look on me, the one they have pierced." Though Yahweh is speaking, this is obviously a reference to Christ's future crucifixion (see Revelation 1:7).[8]

In Isaiah 44:24 Yahweh speaks about His exclusive role in the creation of the universe: "I am the LORD [Yahweh], who has made all things, who alone stretched out the heavens, who spread out the earth by myself." Yet the New Testament just as clearly tells us that Jesus is the agent of creation. "Through him all things were made; without him nothing was made that has been made" (John 1:3; see also Colossians 1:16). This can mean only one thing: Jesus and Yahweh are equated.

Further, Isaiah 40:3 speaks prophetically: "In the desert prepare the way for the Lord *[Yahweh];* make straight in the wilderness a highway for our God *[Elohim]*." Mark's Gospel tells us that Isaiah's words were fulfilled by John the Baptist's work of preparing the way for Jesus (Mark 1:2-4).

In view of these facts, Masons do violence to God's declarations in the Scriptures when they bar the mention of Jesus from the halls of Masonic Lodges.

Jesus once declared that "he who is not with me is against me, and he who does not gather with me scatters" (Matthew 12:30). By refusing to acknowledge

Jesus within Masonic Lodges, Masons are demonstrating that they are not "with" Christ. Help your Mason friend to see the sobering implications of this practice.

 Jesus' words about loving one another cannot be twisted to mean that we should ignore false doctrine. It is true that Jesus was the most loving human being that ever lived. It is also true that one of His primary teachings is that we should love one another—even our enemies (Matthew 5:44). Yet Jesus was not saying we should ignore false doctrine. To the contrary, He often warned His followers about the possibility of spiritual and religious deception:

- "Watch out for false prophets. They come to you in sheep's clothing, but inwardly they are ferocious wolves" (Matthew 7:15,16).

- "Watch out that no one deceives you. For many will come in my name, claiming, 'I am the Christ,' and will deceive many....Many false prophets will appear and deceive many people" (Matthew 24:4,5,11).

Those that Christ criticized most severely during His three-year ministry were the religious leaders of Israel, who were oppressing the common people with religious doctrine. Though Jesus was the most loving person who ever lived, He reserved His most scathing words for these false teachers: "hypocrites," "blind guides," "blind fools," "blind men," and "whitewashed tombs, which look beautiful on the outside but on the inside are full of dead men's bones and everything unclean" (Matthew 23:13,16,17,19,27).

 Ask your Mason friend this: Though Jesus was the most loving person who ever lived, did you know He also sternly warned His followers about false prophets and false Christs? (Be ready to share Matthew 7:15,16 and 24:4,5,11.) Did you know Jesus reserved His harshest words for false religious leaders? (Be ready to share Matthew 23:13-17.)

 Jesus' name should not be stripped from Bible references, especially in view of the clear teaching of Deuteronomy 4:2: "Do not add to what I command you and do not subtract from it, but keep the commands of the LORD your God that I give you." In the same spirit, the apostle John tells us, "I warn everyone who hears the words of the prophecy of this book: If anyone adds anything to them, God will add to him the plagues described in this book. And if anyone takes words away from this book of prophecy, God will take away from him his share in the tree of life and in the holy city, which are described in this book" (Revelation 22:18,19).

Stripping the name of Jesus from Bible verses is especially heinous in view of the fact that all of Scripture *exalts* Jesus. Philippians 2:10,11, for example, tells us that Christ was given a name above every name, "that at the name of Jesus every knee should bow, in heaven and on earth and under the earth, and every tongue confess that Jesus Christ is Lord."

 Since Deuteronomy 4:2 and Revelation 22:18,19 explicitly warn people against adding to or subtracting from God's Word, isn't it dangerous to strip the name of Jesus from Scripture citations? Ask your Mason friend.

 Prayer should be in the name of Jesus. Jesus spoke to His disciples about prayer and said, "I will do whatever you ask *in my name,* so that the Son may bring glory to the Father. You may ask me for anything *in my name,* and I will do it" (John 14:13,14, emphasis added). In John 15:16 Jesus affirmed that "the Father will give you whatever you ask *in my name,*" and in the next chapter (16:23) declared again, "I tell you the truth, my Father will give you whatever you ask *in my name*" (emphasis added to both references).

The reason we must pray in the name of Jesus is given in 1 Timothy 2:5: "There is one God and one mediator between God and men, the man Christ Jesus." To leave Jesus out of the equation is, simply put, to cut oneself off from access to God.

 When prayers are offered in the name of the "Great Architect of the Universe," this means that Hindus and Muslims (and followers of other religions) are interpreting the prayers as being in the name of their own gods, which are pagan deities. No Christian should participate in a prayer in which some of the people present are praying to false gods. Point this out to your Mason friend.

 Jesus died for our sins, not because of His high morality. Jesus "gave himself as a ransom for all men" (1 Timothy 2:6). A "ransom" is something given in exchange for another person or thing—the price of redemption. The idea is that of substitution—Christ taking our place. He died to satisfy the demands of the offended righteousness of God. He died as the sinner's substitute (Matthew 20:28), thus providing a salvation for human beings that they had no hope of procuring for themselves.

It was for the very purpose of dying that Jesus came into the world (John 12:27). Moreover, He declared that His death was a sacrificial offering for the sins of humanity (speaking of His blood being "poured out for many for the forgiveness of sins"— Matthew 26:26-28.) Jesus took His sacrificial mission with utmost seriousness, for He knew that without Him, humanity would certainly perish (Matthew 16:26) and spend eternity apart from God in a place of great suffering (Luke 16:22-28).

In John 10, Jesus compared Himself to a good shepherd who not only gives His life to save the sheep (John 10:11) but lays His life down of His own accord (verse 18). This is precisely what Jesus did at the cross—He laid His life down as a sacrifice for the sins of all people (1 John 2:2).

Isn't it clear from Scripture that Jesus died not because of *His high* morality but because of *our low* morality (that is, He died for our sins in order to make salvation possible)? Be ready to share some of the above Bible verses.

 Jesus is the* only way *of salvation. Jesus claimed that what He said took precedence over the words of all others. He said He is humanity's *only means* of coming into a relationship with God (see John 14:6). This was confirmed by those who followed Him (Acts 4:12; 1 Timothy 2:5). And Jesus warned His followers about those who would try to set forth a different "Christ" (Matthew 24:4,5).

Though God's way of salvation is *narrow* (faith in Christ alone), God's heart is infinitely *wide*. He is full of love for *all* people—men and women, rich and poor, fat and thin, kings and peasants, the social elite and social outcasts (see Ezekiel 18:23; Isaiah 45:22; 1 Timothy 2:3,4). He offers the same gift to everyone—a *unique* gift, the gift of salvation in Jesus Christ. Jesus wants all people to receive this wonderful gift (see Matthew 28:19; John 3:17), as did the apostles (Acts 26:28,29; Romans 1:16). This is the predominant emphasis of Scripture.

 Jesus taught that those who do not honor Him also do not honor the Father who sent Him (John 5:23). The apostle John affirms this: "No one who denies the Son has the Father" (1 John 2:23). And in Luke 9:26 Jesus said: "If anyone is ashamed of me and my words, the Son of Man will be ashamed of him when he comes in his glory and in the glory of the Father and of the holy angels." Ask your Mason friend about the wisdom of deemphasizing Jesus, who is the only way of salvation (John 14:6; Acts 4:12; 1 Timothy 2:5).

The Jesus of Hinduism and the Jesus of Islam are radically different from the Jesus of the Bible, and hence Christians should not worship together with Hindus and Muslims. According to Hinduism, Jesus is one of many holy men who communicated spiritual truth. He certainly was not humankind's only savior, nor was He uniquely the Son of God, nor was He perfect. Rather He was a great master, in a league with other great masters.[9] It is believed there were holy men who were actually greater than Jesus—for example, Prabhupada, who founded the Hare Krishna movement.

Hindus teach that Jesus did not suffer on the cross, for He was a man who had attained enlightenment and was beyond the possibility of physical pain. Maharishi Mahesh Yogi commented, "It's a pity that Christ is talked of in terms of suffering."[10]

 Christianity teaches that Jesus is the unique Son of God (John 3:16), is the only Savior of humankind (John 14:6; Acts 4:12; 1 Timothy 2:5), is perfect in every way (Hebrews 7:26), is exalted above all human beings (Philippians 2:5-11), and did suffer on the cross (Matthew 16:21). Isn't it clear that Hindus and Christians hold radically different views about Jesus? This being so, *how can Christians worship together with Hindus in a Masonic Lodge?* Be sure to ask your Mason friend.

Islam, too, holds a diminished view of Jesus. Muslims believe Jesus was one of the foremost prophets of God, a sinless man who was a messenger of God—bringing truth for His age. But He was not the Son of God. He was not God in human flesh. He is to be honored, but no more so than any other prophet of Allah. He is a lesser prophet than Muhammad.

Muslims say Jesus did not die on the cross, but rather ascended directly into heaven (Judas was crucified in His place). It would have been unthinkable for Allah to have allowed one of his prophets to be crucified. Therefore, the crucifixion of Christ is viewed as a doctrine disrespectful to Allah.

Since Christianity teaches that Jesus is not just a prophet but is God incarnate (John 1:1,18), is exalted above all humans—including Muhammad—(Philippians 2:5-11), and was indeed crucified on the cross (Matthew 27:22-54), isn't it clear that Muslims and Christians hold radically different views about Jesus? This being so, *how can Christians worship together with Muslims in a Masonic Lodge?* Ask your Mason friend.

Jesus Is Not Just a Good Moral Teacher—He Is Uniquely the Son of God

✓ Jesus was more than a moral teacher. He was and is absolute deity.

✓ Jesus' words about loving one another cannot be twisted to mean that we should ignore false doctrine.

✓ Jesus' name should not be stripped from Bible references.

✓ Prayer should be in the name of Jesus.

✓ Jesus died for our sins, not because of His high morality.

✓ Jesus is the only way of salvation.

✓ The Jesus of Hinduism and the Jesus of Islam are radically different from the Jesus of the Bible, and hence Christians should not worship together with Hindus and Muslims.

For further information on the Masonic view of Jesus, consult *Reasoning from the Scriptures with Masons,* pages 151–72.

Salvation

Is Not by Ethical Living—It Is by Faith in Christ

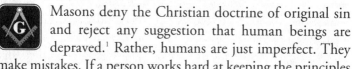 Masons deny the Christian doctrine of original sin and reject any suggestion that human beings are depraved.[1] Rather, humans are just imperfect. They make mistakes. If a person works hard at keeping the principles and teachings of the Masonic Lodge—if he lives *ethically*—he will finally be ushered into the Celestial Lodge Above, where the Supreme Architect of the Universe resides.[2]

The Masonic Lodge advocates that human beings can, in and of themselves, improve their somewhat flawed or unpolished character and behavior and attain the moral perfection necessary to go to heaven.[3] Masonry's purpose is "to make good men better."[4] By ethical living, Masons can "mount by the theological ladder from the Lodge on earth to the Lodge in heaven."[5]

Masons use symbols like the gavel to represent the goal of removing the "rough edges" from our overall good character. Freemasonry allegedly provides what every human being needs to attain moral perfection. This heightened morality is evidenced in the fact that Masons are typically involved in charity and engage in civic duties.

Masonic Symbols

"Masonry uses the Ashlar, Gavel, Square, and Compass—to remind the members that they ever must work out their imperfections in order to be found acceptable to the 'Supreme Grand Master' and to achieve a life in paradise, the 'Grand Lodge Above.'"[6]

The Masonic view of salvation is works-oriented from beginning to end. A man *earns* salvation by living ethically in accordance with whatever holy book he subscribes to (the Christian Bible, the Hindu Vedas, or the Muslim Koran, for example). In this regard, Masons cite James 2:17-26, which emphasizes the need for good works ("faith without works is dead"). As well, Masons say, Jesus in His parable of the Good Samaritan graphically demonstrated the need for good deeds (Luke 10:30-37). In keeping with this, one of the closing prayers used in the lodge includes the words, "May we so practice thy precepts, that we may finally obtain thy promises, and find an entrance through the gates into the temple and city of our God."[7]

Salvation: The Masonic View

- There is no "original sin." Humans are just imperfect.
- Salvation is attained by ethical living.
- Through Masonry, humans can polish their flawed character and attain heaven.
- Man's ethics can be based on *any* holy book.

The Bible teaches that salvation is not by ethical living, but is a grace-gift received through faith in Christ. 1) Man is not just imperfect, but is a sinner; 2) having noble ethics is not enough to attain salvation; 3) the biblical view of salvation involves justification; 4) James 2 does not teach that good works are necessary for salvation; 5) Jesus' parable about the Good Samaritan does not teach that good works are necessary for salvation; and 6) because Christianity's concept of salvation is radically different from that of Hinduism and Islam, Christians should not worship together with Hindus and Muslims.

 Man is not just imperfect, but is a sinner. The Bible indicates that every human being is born into this world in a state of sin. When Adam and Eve sinned, it didn't just affect them alone; it affected the entire human race. The apostle Paul wrote that "sin entered the world through one man, and death through sin, and in this way death came to all men, because all sinned" (Romans 5:12). He asserted that, "through the disobedience of the one man the many were made sinners" (Romans 5:19; see also 1 Corinthians 15:21,22).

In Psalm 51:5 David said, "Surely I was sinful at birth, sinful from the time my mother conceived me." Human beings are born into the world in a state of sin. The sin nature is passed on *from conception.* This is why Ephesians 2:3 says we are "by nature objects of wrath."

This does not mean that every human being is as bad as he or she can be, or commits all the sins that are possible, or is incapable of doing kind and benevolent things to others. What it does mean is that every human is contaminated by sin, and that there is nothing that any human can do to earn merit before a just and holy God.

C.H. Spurgeon once said, "He who doubts human depravity had better study himself."[8] Scripture declares: "There is no one righteous, not even one; there is no one who understands, no one who seeks God. All have turned away....There is no one who does good, not even one" (Romans 3:10-12; see also Isaiah 64:6).

In the words of Jesus, "Out of the heart come evil thoughts, murder, adultery, sexual immorality, theft, false testimony, slander...." (Matthew 15:19). Freemasonry focuses its attention on external ethics; it can do nothing to cure the ills of the *inner* human heart. Only Christ can do that. People do not need a superficial Masonic tune-up, they need a *brand-new engine*. They need to become brand-new creatures (2 Corinthians 5:17), and that can only happen through a personal relationship with Christ that begins at the new birth (John 3:3-5).

God asks, "Can the Ethiopian change his skin or the leopard its spots? Neither can you do good who are accustomed to doing evil" (Jeremiah 13:23). We need a change *from within*. As one writer put it, "According to the Bible, man cannot simply get out the 'Gavel' and knock off the rough edges of human nature. Sin is far more deeply ingrained in man than that. Simply chipping off a few rough edges will not solve the sin problem or give one right standing before God."[9]

 When you talk to your Mason friend, ask: What do you think of C.H. Spurgeon's statement "He who doubts human depravity had better study himself"? Can I share a few Bible verses with you? (Be ready to share Romans 3:10-12, 5:12, and 5:19.)

 Having noble ethics is not enough to attain salvation. If a right relationship with God simply required good ethics, then any religion would do just fine. Hinduism? Islam? Take your pick. After all, the various world religions all provide ethical rules that aim to make human beings into better people. But Christianity paints man's problem as much worse than a mere ethics problem.

The Bible portrays all human beings as spiritually *dead* (dead in "transgressions and sins"—Ephesians 2:1). To put it another way, while the other religions seek to take "good" men (in reality, *bad* men) and make them better, Christianity seeks to take *dead* men and make them *spiritually alive*. There's a universe of difference between the two. If it is true that we are spiritually dead, it means there is nothing we can do to remedy our situation. *Dead people are helpless.* We need help from outside ourselves. And that help has come in Jesus Christ, who died on the cross for our sins and supernaturally makes those who believe in Him spiritually alive, just as if their bodies had been dead and were now resurrected to brand-new life. "If anyone is in Christ, he is a new creation; the old has gone, the new has come!" (2 Corinthians 5:17).

 Tell your Mason friend that it is true that non-Christian religions focus primarily on ethics, seeking to make people better. Christianity, by contrast, seeks to take *dead* people and make them spiritually *alive.* (Be ready to explain what you mean. Focus attention on 2 Corinthians 5:17.)

 The biblical view of salvation involves justification. Contrary to a system of salvation through works, the Bible indicates that we become "justified" the moment we trust in Christ. Biblical justification is a singular and instantaneous event in which God judicially (legally) declares the believing sinner to be absolutely righteous (Romans 3:25,28,30; 8:33,34; Galatians 4:21–5:12; 1 John 1:7–2:2).

Negatively, the word "justification" means a person is once-for-all pronounced *not guilty* before God. He is legally acquitted! Positively, the word means a person is once-for-all pronounced *righteous* before God. The very righteousness of Christ is imputed (or credited) to the believer's life.

This legal declaration is something outside of man. It does not hinge on man's personal level of righteousness. It does not hinge on anything that man does. It hinges solely on God's declaration—His judicial pronouncement. Even while the person is still a sinner and is experientially not righteous, he is nevertheless righteous *in God's sight* because of justification (Romans 3:25,28,30).

The moment one places personal faith in Christ, God makes an incalculable "deposit" of righteousness into one's personal "spiritual bank account." It is a once-for-all transaction on God's part. It is irrevocable, and it cannot be lost. God's pronouncement is final. This is the wonderful gift of salvation.

Romans 3:24 tells us that God's declaration of righteousness is given to believers "freely by his grace." The word *grace* literally means "unmerited favor." It is because of God's unmerited favor that believers receive salvation. This does not mean, however, that God's declaration of righteousness has no objective basis. God did not just subjectively decide to overlook man's sin or wink at his unrighteousness. Rather Jesus died on the cross for us—in our stead—and paid for our sins. He ransomed us from death by His own death on the cross (2 Corinthians 5:21).

There has been a great exchange. As the great reformer Martin Luther said, "Lord Jesus, you are my righteousness, I am your sin. You have taken upon yourself what is mine and given me what is yours. You have become what You were not so that I might become what I was not."[10]

A key blessing that results from being declared righteous is that we now have peace with God (Romans 5:1)—something that a Mason's attempt to live ethically can never give. The Father sees believers through the "lens" of Jesus Christ. And because there is peace between the Father and Jesus, there is also peace between the Father and us believers, since we are "in Christ."

 If a person were to look through a piece of red glass, everything would appear red. If a person were to look through a piece of blue glass, everything would appear blue. If a person were to look through a piece of yellow glass, everything would appear yellow, and so on. Likewise, when we believe in Jesus Christ as our Savior, God looks at us *through the Lord Jesus Christ.*

He sees us in all the pure white holiness of His Son. For this reason, Scripture indicates there is now no condemnation—literally, *no punishment*—for those who are in Christ Jesus (Romans 8:1). Be sure to share this good news with your Mason friend.

The Bible indicates that this gift of justification comes only by faith in Christ, and not by personal works (Romans 4:1-25; Galatians 3:6-14). God justifies "those who have faith in Jesus" (Romans 3:26). Indeed, "a man is justified by faith apart from works of the Law" (Romans 3:28 NASB). By trusting in Christ alone, we are given what we could never earn: a right relationship with God. "Having been justified by faith, we have peace with God through our Lord Jesus Christ" (Romans 5:1).

 Some Masons may object that there are verses in the Bible that seem to indicate the necessity of good works. Point out that good works are a *by-product* of salvation (Matthew 7:15-23; 1 Timothy 5:10,25). They result from the changed purpose for living that salvation brings (1 Corinthians 3:10-15). We are not saved *by* our works, but in order *to do* good works. We do works not to get salvation, but because we have already gotten it. Works are a *consequence* of justification, not a *condition* for it.

James 2 does not teach that good works are necessary for salvation. Though Masons such as Albert Pike argue from James 2 that a man is justified by *what he does* (good works or ethical living), that is not what James is really teaching. In this passage James is basically answering the question, "How can someone tell whether or not a person has true faith?" All that follows in chapter 2 answers this question.

James begins by asking, "What use is it, my brethren, if someone says he has faith but he has no works? Can that faith save him?" (2:14 NASB). Notice the oft-neglected little word "says" ("What use is it, my brethren, if someone *says* he has faith?"). Some people have genuine faith; others have an empty *profession* of faith that is not real. The first group of people, who have genuine faith, have works to back up the fact that their faith is genuine. The second group, those who make an empty profession of faith, show their lack of true faith by the absence of works. So, James answers his question by pointing out that you can tell whether a person has true faith by the test of works. Works are the visible evidences of faith's invisible presence. In other words, good works are the "vital signs" indicating that faith is alive.

Keep in mind that James was writing to Jewish Christians ("to the twelve tribes"—James 1:1) who were in danger of giving nothing but lip-service to Jesus. Apparently some of these Jewish Christians had made a false claim of faith. It is this spurious boast of faith that James was condemning. Merely *claiming* to have faith is insufficient. Genuine faith is evidenced by works. Indeed,

> workless faith is worthless faith; it is unproductive, sterile, barren, dead! Great claims may be made about a corpse that is supposed to have come to life, but if it does not move, if there are no vital signs, no heartbeat, no perceptible pulse, it is still dead. The false claims are silenced by the evidence.[11]

The fact is, apart from the spirit, the body is dead. By analogy, apart from the evidence of good works, faith is dead. It is lifeless and nonproductive. *That* is what James is teaching in these verses. His focus is on the *nature of faith,* not on the *reward of works.*

Jesus' parable about the Good Samaritan does not teach that good works are necessary for salvation. Masons often assert that the true test of religion is the good works that *result from* the religion, and they believe Jesus' parable of the Good Samaritan proves this (Luke 10:30-37). However, this is a misinterpretation of Jesus' words.

This passage deals not with salvation but with how one should treat other people. More precisely, Jesus was teaching that when you see someone in need, and you have the means of helping that person in need, then, like the Good Samaritan, you should help that person. Certainly we can be thankful that Masons are interested in helping other people. However, if the Mason thinks that, by helping other people, he is earning his salvation, then that is wrong. Good works have virtually nothing to do with salvation. Rather, good works *follow* salvation. As we noted previously, we do works not to *get* salvation, but because we have *already gotten* it.

The same Jesus who told the story about the Good Samaritan also consistently taught that it is only by personal faith in Him that a person can be saved:

- "I tell you the truth, whoever hears my word and believes him who sent me has eternal life and will not be condemned; he has crossed over from death to life" (John 5:24).

- "I am the resurrection and the life. He who believes in me will live, even though he dies" (John 11:25).

- "I have come into the world as a light, so that no one who believes in me should stay in darkness" (John 12:46).

 If salvation were not by faith alone, then Jesus' message in the Gospel of John—evidenced in the above quotations—would be deceptive. If righteous works and charitable deeds were necessary for salvation, it would have been deceitful of Jesus to say so many times that there is only one condition for salvation— faith. Help your Mason friend to understand this.

Because Christianity's concept of salvation is radically different from that of Hinduism and Islam, Christians should not worship together with Hindus and Muslims. In Hinduism, the soul and salvation are interpreted in terms of reincarnation. The fate of the soul in each lifetime is said to be governed by the law of *karma*. If one builds up good karma during one's life by performing good works in accord with *dharma* (the moral order of the universe), one will be born in the next life in a favorable state. If one builds up bad karma during one's life, one will be born in the next life in a less desirable state. This goes on life after life after life. The goal is to become increasingly perfect over many lifetimes, break free from the "wheel of karma," and then merge with the universal soul. This is salvation according to Hinduism.

Human effort is also pivotal in the Islamic view of salvation, but in Islam, by contrast, salvation is said to be found in complete surrender to Allah. This is in keeping with the meaning of *Islam* ("submission") and *Muslim* ("one who submits"). Salvation for the Muslim, then, is based on works as well. However, these works are entirely different from those prescribed by Hinduism.

In contrast to both Islam and Hinduism, Christianity teaches that at the moment one trusts in Christ, one is born again (John 3:5), declared righteous (Romans 3:24), reconciled to God (2 Corinthians 5:19), forgiven (Hebrews 10:17), and adopted into God's forever family (Romans 8:14,15). Salvation is a free gift of God received by faith in Jesus Christ (John 3:16; Acts 16:31). The differences between Christianity, Hinduism, and Islam could not be greater.

 Whereas Hinduism teaches that salvation is slowly achieved via reincarnation over many lifetimes, Islam says salvation comes only by complete surrender to Allah. And since *both* of these contradict the biblical view of salvation, how can adherents of each of these religions worship under the same roof together? Help your Mason friend understand the significance of this issue.

Salvation Is Not by Ethical Living—It Is by Faith in Christ

✓ Man is not just imperfect, but is a sinner.

✓ Having noble ethics is not enough to attain salvation.

✓ The biblical view of salvation involves justification.

✓ James 2 does not teach that good works are necessary for salvation.

✓ Jesus' parable about the Good Samaritan does not teach that good works are necessary for salvation.

✓ Christianity, Hinduism, and Islam hold irreconcilable views of salvation. Hence, Christians should not worship together with Hindus and Muslims.

For further information on the Masonic view of salvation, consult *Reasoning from the Scriptures with Masons,* pages 173–206.

8

Masonry

Is Connected to Occultism and Paganism

 Some of the rituals in Freemasonry have a connection with the occult (though perhaps some Masons—particularly Christian Masons—may be unaware of this). Many Masons themselves acknowledge indebtedness to occultism. H.L. Haywood, for example, concedes that "all our historians, at least nearly all of them, agree that Freemasonry owes very much to certain occult societies or groups that flourished—often in secret—during the late Middle Ages..."[1]

The nineteenth through the twenty-eighth degrees of the Scottish Rite involve occultism—including the development of psychic powers, telepathy, altered states of consciousness, mysticism, kabbalism (an occult system that began among the Jewish people about the first century A.D.), Rosicrucianism (a mystical brotherhood involving occult powers and spirit contact), hermetic philosophy (alchemy), and the pursuit of esoteric truths.[2]

Kabbalism is a form of occultism that seems especially prevalent in Masonic circles. It is essentially a mystical system that uses an occultic method of interpreting Scripture. This system espouses the idea that every letter in Scripture contains a mystery that can be solved or interpreted by the initiated.[3]

> ### 🔍 Kabbalism and Syncretism
>
> The kabbalists "were syncretists in believing that at heart all the great religions are practically one, yet they sought to find common ground for Jews, Christians, and Muslims."[4] The similarity to Masonry is obvious.

Masons are quite open about the connection between Freemasonry and the kabbala. Albert Pike confesses that "the Kabbala is the key of the occult sciences."[5] He sees kabbalism in Masonry at every turn, which is why he encourages the Mason to familiarize himself with kabbalistic doctrine.[6] Albert Mackey likewise says that "much use is made of it in the advanced [Masonic] degrees, and entire rites have been constructed on its principles. Hence it demands a place in any general work on Masonry."[7]

To be fair, the Mason who joins the Blue Lodge and considers it *just* a fraternal organization may be completely unaware of much of the occultism practiced in the Lodge. In fact, Christian apologists John Ankerberg and John Weldon have commented that

> most Masons who participate in the rituals do not understand their occult significance. If they pursue Masonry no further than unthinking participation in the rituals, it may be true for them that Masonry is not occultic. Such Masons are unaware of the occult meaning of many of the Masonic symbols and ritual and have chosen not to pursue the issue. But this is not true for all Masons. Others do pursue the occult significance of Masonry.[8]

There is also a connection between Freemasonry and the mystery religions of paganism. In reading Masonic literature one often comes across references to Egyptian deities connected with one or another of the ancient mystery religions. Some Masonic authorities have written about how Masonic ritual is rooted in and has borrowed from some of these ancient mysteries.[9]

Isis, Serapis, and *Osiris* are pagan deities of the ancient Egyptian mystery religions that are mentioned regularly in Masonic literature.[10] Other Egyptian deities, such as the great sun god *Re, Apis* (the sacred bull god), *Thoth, Ptah, Hermes, Orpheus,* and *Horus,* among others, are also regularly cited.[11] Albert Pike makes mention of "the 12 great gods of Egypt."[12] Not surprisingly, he suggests that Masonry is "a successor of the mysteries," and is "identical with the ancient mysteries."[13] Vindex likewise writes that Freemasonry is "the heir and legitimate successor of the ancient mysteries."[14] In the *Holy Bible— Masonic Edition,* we read, "It is admitted that Masonry is descended from the ancient mysteries."[15]

Though my historical research indicates that there is no *direct historical lineage* from the ancient mystery religions to the Freemasonry of today, it does seem clear that modern Masonry has borrowed many of its ideas and rituals from these ancient religions.[16] These mystery religions stressed oaths of secrecy, secret rites of initiation, brotherhood, religious quests, and immortality. They worshiped and engaged in rituals involving numerous pagan deities, and promoted occultism of various sorts.[17] Although it is not clear how and precisely when Freemasonry assimilated ideas from ancient mystery religions, it seems likely that some of the occult groups of the Middle Ages (and after) influenced Freemasonry in this regard.[18]

Freemasonry, Occultism, and Paganism

- There is an occult connection between Freemasonry and occultism.

- There is also a connection between Freemasonry and ancient mystery religions.

- Although there is no direct historical lineage from the ancient mystery religions to modern Freemasonry, Masons have borrowed key ideas from these ancient religions.

The Bible condemns all involvement in the occult and in pagan religions. 1) God condemns *all* forms of occultism; 2) the true source of occultism is Satan; 3) the gods of paganism are *false* gods that do not really exist; and 4) repentance is in order for any Christian who has participated in an organization that espouses false gods and involvement in the occult.

 God condemns all forms of occultism, most notably in Deuteronomy 18:9-12, where we are told that all such things are detestable to God:

> When you enter the land the LORD your God is giving you, do not learn to imitate the detestable ways of the nations there. Let no one be found among you who sacrifices his son or daughter in the fire, who practices divination or sorcery, interprets omens, engages in witchcraft, or casts spells, or who is a medium or spiritist or who consults the dead. Anyone who does these things is detestable to the LORD, and because of these detestable practices the LORD your God will drive out those nations before you.

God's stand against occultism and divination is consistent throughout Scripture. Exodus 22:18 instructs that sorceresses are to be put to death, a penalty that demonstrates how serious the sin of divination is. God commands, "Do not practice divination or sorcery....Do not turn to mediums or seek out spiritists, for you will be defiled by them" (Leviticus 19:26,31). Then we read again of the penalty, in Leviticus 20:27: "A man or woman who is a medium or spiritist among you must be put to death." First Samuel 28:3 reports that King Saul rightly "expelled the mediums and spiritists from the land," but a later writer tells us that "Saul died because he was unfaithful to the LORD; he did not keep the word of the LORD and even consulted a medium for guidance" (1 Chronicles 10:13). In Acts 19:19 we read that many who converted to Christ in the city of

Ephesus rightly destroyed all the paraphernalia they had formerly used for divination and other occult practices.

 Should a person remain in the Masonic Lodge despite the fact that God *condemns* the occultism that is a part of the Lodge? Should a person have one foot in God's kingdom and the other in Satan's? Help your Mason friend to weigh his eternal priorities.

 The true source of occultism is Satan. Scripture reveals a great deal about this evil being. One aspect of Satan's character and activity that is very closely connected with the topic of this chapter is his work of *deception*. He is called the "father of lies" (John 8:44). The word "father" is used here metaphorically—that is, Satan is the *originator* of a family or company of persons who are animated by deceitful character. He was the first and greatest liar. Consider these points:

- It is a lie to say that the God of Christianity is the same as the god of Hinduism and the god of Islam.

- It is a lie to say that God's true name is "Jabulon"—a name that associates the biblical God with Baal and Osiris, corrupt pagan deities of the ancient world.

- It is a lie to say that Jesus was just a good, moral teacher.

- It is a lie to say that man has no sin nature and can therefore perform good works sufficient to merit the Celestial Lodge Above.

- It is a lie to say that the Bible can be understood by using kabbalistic esoteric methodology.

These and other such ideas are without doubt rooted in the work of Satan, the father of lies.

In keeping with his work of deception, Satan may be viewed as the great counterfeiter.[19] It was Augustine who called the devil *simius Dei*—"the ape of God." Satan apes or mimics God in many ways. (Second Corinthians 11:14 affirms that Satan is a master of masquerade.) In what ways does Satan act as "the ape of God"? Consider the following—

- Satan has his own church—the "synagogue of Satan" (Revelation 2:9).

- Satan has his own ministers—ministers of darkness that bring false sermons (2 Corinthians 11:3,4).

- Satan has formulated his own system of theology—called "doctrines of demons" (1 Timothy 4:1; Revelation 2:24).

- His ministers proclaim his gospel—"a gospel other than the one we preached to you" (Galatians 1:7,8).

- Satan has his own throne (Revelation 13:2) and his own worshipers (13:4).

- Satan inspires false Christs and self-constituted messiahs (Matthew 24:4,5).

- Satan employs false teachers who bring in "destructive heresies" (2 Peter 2:1).

- Satan sends out false prophets (Matthew 24:11).

- Satan sponsors false apostles who imitate the true ones (2 Corinthians 11:13-15).

In view of this mimicry, one theologian has concluded that "Satan's plan and purposes have been, are, and always will be to seek to establish a rival rule to God's kingdom. He is promoting a system of which he is the head and which stands in opposition to God and His rule in the universe."[20]

This is particularly relevant to our subject matter, for the God of Masonry is a *counterfeit God,* the Jesus of Masonry is a *counterfeit Jesus,* and the gospel of Masonry is a *counterfeit gospel.* Furthermore, Masonry offers a counterfeit system of interpreting the Bible—kabbalism.

We know that Satan is constantly about the business of misinterpreting God's Word and causing human beings to do the same. In the Garden of Eden, Satan, in the form of a serpent, deceptively asked Eve, "Did God really say...?" (Genesis 3:1).

The fall of humankind was the result of that encounter. Satan also twisted Scripture when tempting Jesus, but did not succeed in deceiving the Lord (see Matthew 4:1-11). Satan's desire is to get people to believe that the Bible says something *other* than what it actually and plainly says. Kabbalism is a satanic masterpiece in this regard.

 The Scripture-twisting interpretive methodology of kabbalism is compatible with such deceptions as: 1) All religions worship the same God; 2) Jesus is just a good, moral teacher; 3) man does not have a sin problem; and 4) salvation can be attained by good works. Help your Mason friend see that one of Satan's goals is to get people to believe that the Bible says something *other* than what it actually says. Show him what the Bible really says about God, Jesus, man's sin, and God's grace-gift of salvation by faith in Christ.

 The gods of paganism are* false *gods that do not really exist. Relevant to our present study is this fact: The worship of such deities as Re, Apis, Isis, Osiris, Serapis, and others was judged by God in history. The ten plagues inflicted on the Egyptians by God through Moses served as a judgment against these gods, whom the Egyptians worshiped (see Exodus 12:12). Since that is the case, this means that Freemasons, in their ritual, have borrowed heavily from a false religious system that was condemned and punished horrifically by the one true God.

He—the God of the Bible, whose name is Yahweh—is incomparable. There is no one like Him. Masons desperately need to see that the one true God has no rival, and that the mystery religions they cite in support of their ritual are "dead in the water" before Him.

God's incomparability is expressed in two different ways in the account of the plagues against Egypt. The more common way is by *negation*. Moses' words "There is no one like the LORD our God" exemplify this (Exodus 8:10). Having been exposed to all of the gods of Egypt during his childhood, Moses was surely qualified to make such judgments, especially after experiencing the miraculous manifestation of Yahweh's superior power during the exodus (and later of course).

A second way Moses expressed the incomparability of Yahweh was through rhetorical questions. He often asked, "Who among the gods is like you, O LORD?" (Exodus 15:11). The implied answer is, "No one in all the universe."

In Egyptian religion, the god at the very top of the totem pole was the sun god, *Re*. Next in line was the Pharaoh of Egypt, who was considered to be the son of Re.[21] Hence, the Pharaoh of Egypt was considered a god in his own right. Because Re was seen as superior to all other gods, his son—the Pharaoh—was also considered to possess unmatched power as a god. This adds a whole new dimension to the Exodus account. It is as if a *contest* occurs between the true God on the one side and the false gods of Egypt's mystery religions on the other side (see Numbers 33:4).

The incomparability of Yahweh is magnificently displayed in Exodus 7–11. We can sum up the passage this way: Pharaoh wouldn't listen to God's message, so God inflicted ten miraculous plagues upon Egypt to get his attention.

It all started like this. Moses and Aaron appeared before Pharaoh and confronted him on behalf of Yahweh about the redemption of His people: "This is what the LORD, the God of Israel, says: 'Let my people go, so that they may hold a festival to me in the desert'" (Exodus 5:1). Pharaoh then asked the question of the century: "Who is the LORD [Yahweh] that I should obey him and let Israel go?" (Exodus 5:2). Yahweh answered in full, getting Pharaoh's attention by sending ten plagues and demonstrating that He was (and is) the only true God in the face of all the false deities of Egypt.

This becomes abundantly clear even if we look at only a few of the plagues. For instance, in the first plague, God through Moses turned the Nile River into blood (Exodus 7:17-21). This plague constituted a judgment against the Egyptian sacred river god, *Nilus.*[22] Since Nilus was worshiped by every Egyptian, this plague struck at the very heart of Egyptian religion.

The second plague resulted in a massive swarm of frogs (see 8:1-15). In Egyptian culture frogs were thought to be gods and were venerated. In fact, the intentional killing of a frog was punishable by death.[23] It must have been abhorrent to the Egyptians that everywhere they stepped, they crushed a frog.

Then the ninth plague brought darkness that enveloped the land of Egypt for three days (10:21,22). This judgment was clearly against the sun god Re, the creator, father, and king of the gods. The miraculous plague of darkness in the land crushed the strongest god in Egypt.

By inflicting these ten plagues, Yahweh demonstrated to the Egyptians that He alone is God. There is no one like Him. The Pharaoh *asked* the question "Who is Yahweh?"—Yahweh *answered* the question and left no room for misunderstanding: "By this you will know that I am the LORD" (Exodus 7:17; see also 7:5; 9:14; 10:2).

When we see how often Masonic literature makes reference to the Egyptian deities, it becomes clear that Masons have borrowed heavily from a false religious system that was judged definitively by the one true God of the Bible. Masons must take to heart the words that God spoke to Pharaoh—"I am the LORD."

 Ask your Mason friend: Did you know that when God, through Moses, inflicted the ten plagues upon Egypt, He was actually judging false Egyptian gods? What do you think these judgments indicate about the true God's attitude toward false Egyptian deities? Since Masonic literature regularly makes reference to these deities, what do you think the true God's attitude is toward the Lodge?

 Repentance is in order for any Christian who has participated in an organization that espouses false gods and involvement in the occult. In 2 Corinthians 6:14-17 the apostle Paul sternly wrote,

Do not be yoked together with unbelievers. For what do righteousness and wickedness have in common? Or what fellowship can light have with darkness? What harmony is there between Christ and Belial? What does a believer have in common with an unbeliever? What agreement is there between the temple of God and idols? For we are the temple of the living God. As God has said: "I will live with them and walk among them, and I will be their God, and they will be my people." "Therefore come out from them and be separate, says the Lord. Touch no unclean thing, and I will receive you."

What Masons have done in bringing the false gods of Egypt into their ritual is an outrage to the true God's holy name. God's message—not just to Masons, but to all people everywhere—is this: *There is none like Me in all the earth; therefore, come out from them and be separate, says the Lord God Almighty.*

 Ask your Mason friend: Would you please open your Bible and read out loud from 2 Corinthians 6:14-17? Do you think you should reconsider your involvement in the Masonic Lodge?

 Masonry Is Connected to Occultism and Paganism

✓ God condemns *all* forms of occultism.

✓ The true source behind occultism is Satan.

✓ The gods of paganism are *false* gods that do not really exist.

✓ Repentance is in order for any Christian who has participated in an organization that espouses false gods and involvement in the occult.

 For further information on the connection between Freemasonry and occultism–paganism, consult *Reasoning from the Scriptures with Masons*, pages 131–49, 225–34.

Christians

Should Not Participate in Masonry

 In 1992, Southern Baptist James Holly requested that the Southern Baptist Convention (SBC) conduct an investigation of Freemasonry. The SBC agreed, and in June of 1993 published its findings—the "Freemasonry Report." The report begins by commending the Masonic Order for its many charitable endeavors, including the operation of numerous hospitals, burn centers, and a foundation for the prevention of drug and alcohol abuse among children.[1] Yet the report also spoke of problems, noting that many tenets and teachings of Freemasonry are not compatible with Christianity or Southern Baptist doctrine, including

> The prevalent use of offensive concepts, titles, and terms such as Worshipful Master for the leader of a lodge; references to their buildings as mosques, shrines, or temples; and the use of words such as Abaddon and Jah-Bul-On, the so-called secret name of God. To many, these terms are not only offensive but sacrilegious.

> ...The use of archaic, offensive rituals and so-called bloody oaths or obligations, among these being that promised by the Entered Apprentice.

...The reference to the Bible placed on the altar of the lodge as the furniture of the lodge, comparing it to the square and compass rather than giving it the supreme place in the lodge.

...The implication that salvation may be attained by one's good works, implicit in the statement found in some Masonic writings that Masonry is continually reminded of that purity of life and conduct which is necessary to obtain admittance into the Celestial Lodge Above where the Supreme Architect of the Universe presides.

...The heresy of Universalism (the belief all people will eventually be saved), which permeates the writings of many Masonic authors, which is a doctrine inconsistent with New Testament teaching.

...The refusal of most lodges (although not all) to admit for membership African-Americans.[2]

Despite its recognition of these problems intrinsic to the Masonic Lodge, the report concluded:

In light of the fact that many tenets and teachings of Freemasonry are not compatible with Christianity and Southern Baptist doctrine, while others are compatible with Christianity and Southern Baptist doctrine, we therefore recommend that consistent with our denomination's deep convictions regarding the priesthood of the believer and the autonomy of the local church, membership in a Masonic Order be a matter of personal conscience.[3]

This evaluation by the Southern Baptist Convention has essentially served as an endorsement of the Masonic Lodge. In the *Scottish Rite Journal*, a Masonic periodical, one Mason wrote: "Because of your support, the vote of the Southern Baptist Convention is a historic and positive turning point for Freemasonry. Basically, it is a vitalization of our Fraternity by America's largest Protestant denomination after nearly a year of thorough, scholarly study."[4]

Should Christians Be Masons?

- The Southern Baptist report noted many doctrinal incompatibilities between Freemasonry and Christianity.

- Yet the report concluded that membership in a Masonic Lodge is a matter of individual conscience.

- This report essentially served as an endorsement of Freemasonry.

There are substantive reasons why Christians should not participate in Freemasonry. 1) Many of the rituals and doctrines of Freemasonry are incompatible with Christianity; 2) in view of such incompatibilities, making membership in the Masonic Lodge a matter of individual conscience is unwise; 3) Christian involvement in Freemasonry involves compromise; and 4) numerous Christian denominations and other religious organizations have rightfully taken a public stand against Freemasonry.

Many of the rituals and doctrines of Freemasonry are incompatible with Christianity. It is one thing to join up with a Masonic Lodge because of biblical illiteracy. But once a Christian becomes aware of the problems in Freemasonry's rituals and doctrines, that Christian is confronted with a decision: "Shall I remain in the Masonic Lodge, despite the fact that I know its teachings contradict and subvert God's Word? Or shall I break my oath and leave the Masonic Lodge, thus honoring the one true God?"

Helping your friend make the right decision may become easier if you go over with him the problems discussed in this book. Here are the points you will want to thoroughly review with your Masonic acquaintance.

- When the candidate is undergoing the initiation ceremony, *he is made to stand before the Worshipful Master and say something like: "I am lost in darkness, and I am seeking the light of Freemasonry."*[5] This is the case even for the Christian who has already been delivered from the kingdom of darkness into the kingdom of light (Ephesians 5:8-11).

- When the candidate is undergoing the initiation ceremony, *he is made to swear a blood oath,* saying, "Binding myself under no less penalty than that of having my throat cut across, my tongue torn out by its roots, and my body buried in the rough sands of the sea...should I ever knowingly violate this my Entered Apprentice obligation."[6] No Christian has any business taking such an oath.

- *The candidate is taught that the Bible is not God's only revelation to humankind,* but is simply one of many holy books that contain religious and moral truth. The Bible is said to be just a symbol of God's will.[7] Other "revelatory" books include the Hindu Vedas and the Muslim Koran.

- *The candidate is taught that Jews, Christians, Hindus, Muslims, and those of other faiths are all worshiping the same God using different names.* God is said to be "the nameless one of a hundred names."[8] This tenet is held despite the fact that Christianity teaches a triune concept of God, Islam denies the Trinity and says God cannot have a son, and Hinduism involves virtually millions of gods.

- *God's true name is said to be "Jabulon"*—a name that associates the God of the Bible with Baal and Osiris, ancient pagan deities. Baal worship in particular is the epitome of evil idol worship in the ancient world and involved such things as ritual prostitution (Judges 2:17; Hosea 4:13,14), self-mutilation (1 Kings 18:28), and the sacrificing (ritual murder) of little children (Jeremiah 19:4,5).

- *Freemasonry has strong connections to the ancient mystery religions,* and often cites such false gods as Isis, Serapis, Osiris, Re, Apis, Thoth, Ptah, Hermes, Orpheus, and Horus.[9] These are the very gods that the true God Yahweh condemned and judged when inflicting the ten plagues on Egypt through the hand of Moses (see Exodus 7–12).

- *Jesus is often viewed not as God but as no more than a good, moral teacher.* His name is systematically stripped from prayers and from Scripture verses cited within the Masonic Lodge. By contrast, the Bible not only asserts the absolute deity of Christ (John 1:1; 8:58; 10:30; 20:28; Colossians 2:9), but tells us we should always pray in His name (John 16:24). Further, Christ Himself affirmed, "If anyone is ashamed of me and my words, the Son of Man will be ashamed of him when he comes in his glory and in the glory of the Father and of the holy angels" (Luke 9:26).

- *Man is viewed as not being sinful or born into the world with original sin.* Rather, he is viewed as basically good with a few imperfections. This is so despite the fact that Scripture says man is fallen in sin and even his good acts are like filthy rags before God (Isaiah 64:6; see also Isaiah 53:5,6; Romans 3:23; 5:12).

- *Man is said to be saved not by trusting in Christ* but by engaging in good works and charitable acts. This plainly goes against the clear teaching of Scripture (see John 3:16; Acts 16:31; Romans 3:20-22; Ephesians 2:8,9).

- *Masonry involves various forms of occultism in its literature and rituals*—including kabbalism, Rosicrucianism, and alchemy. Scripture, by contrast, condemns all forms of occultism as detestable to God (Deuteronomy 18:10-12; see also Leviticus 19:31; 20:6; Jeremiah 27:9; Micah 5:12).

After going over the above summary, ask your Mason friend: Why not take some time to reflect on all this, and weigh your eternal priorities? Let him know you'll be praying for him.

In view of such incompatibilities, making membership in the Masonic Lodge a matter of individual conscience is unwise. Apologists George Mather and Larry Nichols point out that the Jehovah's Witnesses hold to many "tenets and teachings...not compatible with Christianity and Southern Baptist doctrine [for example, denial of the Trinity, the deity of Christ, bodily resurrection, and so on], while others are compatible [for example, belief in the inspiration and inerrancy of Scripture; a personal God; emphasis on honesty, integrity, industry, character; and so on]." Mather and Nichols thus ask: "Why, then, don't Southern Baptists allow participation and cooperation with the Witnesses 'as a matter of personal conscience'?"[10] They raise a good point.

Ask your Mason friend: Did you know that the Jehovah's Witnesses hold many tenets and teachings not compatible with Christianity and Southern Baptist doctrine, while others are compatible? (Share the compatibilities and incompatibilities.) If it's okay to join a Masonic Lodge even in the face of the severe doctrinal problems intrinsic to Freemasonry, then why not worship alongside Jehovah's Witnesses, or Mormons, or other cultists?

Christian involvement in Freemasonry involves compromise. Christian author Walton Hannah writes, "I am firmly convinced that for a Christian to pledge himself to a religious (or even, to avoid begging the question, to a quasi-religious) organization which offers prayer and worship to God which deliberately excludes the name of our

Lord and Savior Jesus Christ, in whose name only is salvation to be found, is apostatic."[11] He suggests that this apostasy is something the early Christians in the first century would have never succumbed to. "Christians in those days were willing to face death rather than cast a few grains of incense to the Emperor or other deities."[12]

The apostle Paul says we should not fellowship with those who are disobedient to God: "Do not be partners with them. For you were once darkness, but now you are light in the Lord. Live as children of light (for the fruit of the light consists in all goodness, righteousness and truth) and find out what pleases the Lord. Have nothing to do with the fruitless deeds of darkness, but rather expose them" (Ephesians 5:7-10).

Elsewhere, Paul instructs us, "The sacrifices of pagans are offered to demons, not to God, and I do not want you to be participants with demons. You cannot drink the cup of the Lord and the cup of demons too; you cannot have a part in both the Lord's table and the table of demons. Are we trying to arouse the Lord's jealousy?" (1 Corinthians 10:20-22). This applies directly to Masonry, for Masonry involves Christians worshiping together with Muslims and Hindus, which are pagan religions that invoke false deities. Paul said this cannot be. He commands:

> Do not be yoked together with unbelievers. For what do righteousness and wickedness have in common? Or what fellowship can light have with darkness? What harmony is there between Christ and Belial? What does a believer have in common with an unbeliever? What agreement is there between the temple of God and idols? For we are the temple of the living God. As God has said: "I will live with them and walk among them, and I will be their God, and they will be my people." "Therefore come out from them and be separate, says the Lord. Touch no unclean thing, and I will receive you" (2 Corinthians 6:14-17).

In Isaiah 52:11 the followers of the one true God are exhorted: "Touch no unclean thing! Come out from it and be pure." Just as Israel was to abstain from participating with any pagan religions or heathenism, so those of us who call ourselves Christians are to abstain from such things. To worship in Lodges alongside of Hindus and Muslims and those of other religions is to engage in compromise that invites God's judgment.

 Ask your Mason friend how he interprets the apostle Paul's words "Do not be yoked together with unbelievers" (2 Corinthians 6:14). Then ask him this: Don't you think Paul would have considered worshiping alongside of Hindus and Muslims to be yoking oneself together with unbelievers?

 Numerous Christian denominations and other religious organizations have rightfully taken a public stand against Freemasonry, including the Methodist Church of England, the Wesleyan Church, the Russian Orthodox Church, the Roman Catholic Church, the Synod Anglican Church of England, the Assemblies of God, the Church of the Nazarene, the Orthodox Presbyterian Church, the Reformed Presbyterian Church, the Christian Reformed Church in America, the Evangelical Mennonite Church, the Church of Scotland, the Free Church of Scotland, General Association of Regular Baptist Churches, Grace Brethren, Independent Fundamentalist Churches of America, the Evangelical Lutheran Synod, the Baptist Union of Scotland, the Lutheran Church Missouri Synod, the Wisconsin Evangelical Lutheran Synod, and the Presbyterian Church in America.[13]

 If your Masonic acquaintance claims to be a Christian, ask him to reconsider his commitment in view of the near-universal "thumbs down" Freemasonry has received from Christian denominations.

I have long had tremendous respect for Dwight L. Moody, one of this country's most fruitful evangelists of times past. His words on leaving and staying out of the Masonic Lodge are stirring and challenging. I can think of no more appropriate way to sum up this issue than to quote this great man.

> I do not see how any Christian, most of all a Christian minister, can go into these secret lodges with unbelievers. They say they can have more influence for good; but I say they can have more influence for good by staying out of them, and then reproving their evil deeds. You can never reform anything by unequally yoking yourself with ungodly men. True reformers separate themselves from the world. "But," you say, "you had one of them in your church." So I had, but when I found out what it was I cleaned it out like a cage of unclean birds. [Here Moody was referring to a secret temperance union.]
>
> "But Mr. Moody," some say, "if you talk that way you will drive all the members of secret societies out of your meetings and out of your churches." But what if I did? Better men will take their places. Give them the truth anyway, and if they would rather leave their churches than their lodges, the sooner they get out of the churches the better. I would rather have ten members who are separated from the world than a thousand such members. Come out from the lodge. Better one with God, than a thousand without him. We must walk with God, and if only one or two go with us, it is all right. Do not let down the standard to suit men who love their secret lodges or have some darling sin they will not give up.[14]

Christians Should Not Participate in Freemasonry

✓ The rituals and doctrines of Freemasonry are incompatible with Christianity.

✓ In view of such incompatibilities, making membership in the Masonic Lodge a matter of individual conscience is unwise.

✓ Christian involvement in Freemasonry involves compromise.

✓ Numerous Christian denominations and other religious organizations have rightfully taken a public stand against Freemasonry.

 For further information regarding why Christians should not be Masons, consult *Reasoning from the Scriptures with Masons,* pages 235-46.

Jesus
Has Changed
My Life Forever

O ne of the ten most important things to say to a Mason
should be an account of what Jesus has done in your
life—especially pertaining to the grace-gift of salvation
He has given you. Giving your testimony—your personal
story—is an important component of any witnessing encounter.

In my own case, throughout my childhood and teenage years
I thought I was a Christian because I regularly attended church.
For years I participated in various church activities, sang in the
church choir, and went through all the motions. I even went
through a confirmation ceremony at my church—an event that
was supposed to *confirm* I was a Christian. I had no idea at that
time that I really was not a Christian according to the biblical
definition of the term.

Like so many others today, I was under the illusion that a
Christian was a church-attender, or one who basically sub-
scribed to a Christian code of ethics. I believed that as long as I
was fairly consistent in living my life in accordance with this
code of ethics, I was surely a Christian. I believed that as long
as my good deeds outweighed my bad deeds by the time I died,
I could look forward to a destiny in heaven.

It was not until years later I came to understand that the mere act of going to church did not make me a Christian. As the great evangelist Billy Sunday (1862–1935) put it, "Going to church doesn't make you a Christian any more than going to a garage makes you an automobile."[1]

Most fundamentally, a Christian is one who has a personal, ongoing relationship with Jesus. It is a relationship that begins the moment one places faith in Christ for salvation. It has been well said that Christianity is not so much a *religion* as it is a *relationship*.

The word "Christian" is actually used only three times in the New Testament—the most important being in Acts 11:26 (see also Acts 26:28 and 1 Peter 4:16). It is instructive to observe what this word meant among those to whom the term was originally applied. By so doing, we can see whether we are Christians according to the way the Bible itself defines the term.

In Acts 11:26, we are told simply and straightforwardly that "the disciples were called Christians first at Antioch." This would have been around A.D. 42, about a decade after Christ died on the cross and rose from the dead.

What does the term mean? The answer is found in the "ian" ending—for among the ancients this ending meant "belonging to the party of." "Herodians" belonged to the party of Herod. "Caesarians" belonged to the party of Caesar. "Christians" belonged to Christ. And Christians were loyal to Christ, just as the Herodians were loyal to Herod and Caesarians were loyal to Caesar (see Matthew 22:16; Mark 3:6; 12:13).

The significance of the name *Christian* was that these followers of Jesus were recognized as a distinct group. Their party was seen as distinct from Judaism and as distinct from all other religions of the ancient world. We might loosely translate the term Christian as "those belonging to Christ," "Christ-ones," or perhaps "Christ-people." *They are ones who follow Christ.*

Try to imagine what it may have been like in Antioch as one local resident talked to another about these followers of Jesus: "Who are these people?" the one Antiochan might ask—and the other would reply, "Oh, these are the people who are always talking about Christ—the Christ-people, the Christians."

Scholars have noted that the Antiochans were well known for making fun of others. It may be that the early followers of Jesus were called "Christians" as a term of derision or ridicule. But history reveals that, by the second century, Christians had adopted the title as a badge of honor. They took pride (healthy pride) in following Jesus. They had a genuine relationship with the living, resurrected Christ.

I bring all this up because a pivotal part of your personal testimony to a Mason must be the fact that you are sure of going to heaven precisely because you have a personal relationship with Christ. You have meaning in your present life not because you obey rules, or have high ethical standards, but because you *know Jesus*.

Great Christians throughout church history have always emphasized that Christianity most fundamentally involves such a personal relationship.

- Josiah Strong (1847–1916) said, "Christianity is neither a creed nor a ceremonial, but life vitally connected with a loving Christ."[2]

- John R.W. Stott (born 1921) wrote, "A Christian is, in essence, somebody personally related to Jesus Christ."[3]

- Oswald Chambers (1874–1917) said, "Christianity is not devotion to work, or to a cause, or a doctrine, but devotion to a person, the Lord Jesus Christ."[4]

- Billy Graham (born 1918) declared, "Christianity isn't only going to church on Sunday. It is living twenty-four hours of every day with Jesus Christ."[5]

Having laid this basic foundation, I now want to give you a few pointers to keep in mind in regard to testimonies. These pointers are the very things I keep in mind when I tell people what the Lord has done in my own life.

 There is a strong biblical precedent for God's people telling others about what God has done in their lives, and we are to follow the examples given in the Bible:

- "Give thanks to the LORD, call on his name; make known among the nations what he has done" (1 Chronicles 16:8).

- "Tell of all his wonderful acts" (1 Chronicles 16:9).

- "Proclaim among the nations what he has done" (Psalm 9:11).

- "Whoever acknowledges me before men, I will also acknowledge him before my Father in heaven" (Matthew 10:32).

- "Jesus...said, 'Go home to your family and tell them how much the Lord has done for you, and how he has had mercy on you.' So the man went away and began to tell in the Decapolis how much Jesus had done for him. And all the people were amazed" (Mark 5:19,20).

- "Leaving her water jar, the woman went back to the town and said to the people, 'Come, see a man who told me everything I ever did. Could this be the Christ?' They came out of the town and made their way toward him....Many of the Samaritans from that town believed in him because of the woman's testimony, 'He told me everything I ever did'" (John 4:28-31,39).

- "Do not be ashamed to testify about our Lord" (2 Timothy 1:8).

- "Always be prepared to give an answer to everyone who asks you to give the reason for the hope that you have. But do this with gentleness and respect" (1 Peter 3:15).

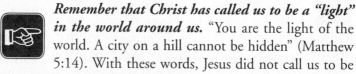

Remember that Christ has called us to be a "light" in the world around us. "You are the light of the world. A city on a hill cannot be hidden" (Matthew 5:14). With these words, Jesus did not call us to be "secret agent" Christians. We are not to cloak our lights. Someone once said, "No one is a light unto himself, not even the sun."[6] Because the darkness of cults and false religions is hovering over Western culture as never before, there has never been a time when the "light" of each Christian has been more needed. As Billy Graham put it, "The Christian should stand out like a sparkling diamond."[7]

How You Live Is Important

Keep in mind that it is not just our words that serve as a witness for Jesus. Our actions, too, serve as a witness. What we *believe* as Christians has an effect on the way we *live*. Don't just share the *facts* of your relationship with Jesus with a Mason; let him see the *effects* of that relationship in your life.

We are called to be personal witnesses about Jesus Christ specifically. Just before ascending into heaven Jesus instructed His disciples: "You will receive power when the Holy Spirit has come upon you; and you shall be My witnesses both in Jerusalem, and in all Judea and Samaria, and even to the remotest part of the earth" (Acts 1:8 NASB). A *witness* is a person who gives testimony. Christians testify *about Jesus*—who He is, what He has done, and their personal relationship with Him.

A Christian leader once said, "Every heart *with* Christ is a missionary; every heart *without* Christ is a mission field." We can be missionaries to Masons wherever we encounter them. We must always be ready to share the good news.

 When you tell others what the Lord has done in your life, speak with conviction. You may not be an authority about what every single verse in the Bible says, but you *are* an authority on what Jesus has personally done in your life. In our day of relativism—a day in which there is so much confusion about so many things—a testimony delivered with conviction will be noticed (see Acts 2:32; 3:15; 4:33; 13:30,31).

 Be careful not to have a "spiritual chip" on your shoulder when you give your testimony. A "spiritual chip" is the communication of the feeling that you are looking down on the Mason because you have something he or she does not have. Such an attitude will turn him or her off as fast as anything you can imagine.[8]
Especially for Christians who have thoroughly prepared themselves by learning hard-hitting scriptural answers to Masonic errors, the temptation may be to *talk down to* the Mason instead of *conversing with* the Mason. Do not let this happen. Be on your guard and make every effort, with God's help, to remain humble during your witnessing encounter. Watch out for spiritual pride; it is deadly!

 When giving your testimony, be sure to share what your life was like before you were a Christian, how you became a Christian, and what your life has been like since becoming a Christian.

- Describe what your life was like before you were a Christian. What were your feelings, attitudes, actions, and relationships like during this time? (The apostle Paul clearly spoke of what his life was like before he was a Christian in Acts 26:4-11.)

- What events happened in your life that led you to your decision to trust in Christ? What caused you to begin considering Christ as a solution to your needs? Was there a crisis? A lack of meaning in life? Be specific.

- Describe your conversion experience. Was it a book you read? Were you in a church? Were other Christians with you at the time? (The apostle Paul straightforwardly told how he became a Christian in Acts 26:12-18.)

- What kind of change took place in your life following your conversion? What effect did trusting in Christ have on your feelings, attitudes, actions, and relationships? (Paul spoke of how his life changed once he became a Christian in Acts 26:19-23.)

 There are certain things you should avoid when sharing your personal testimony.

- *Do not be long-winded.* People have short attention spans. Unless they indicate they want every detail, try to cover the essential points briefly.

- *Try not to use "Christianese" language.* In other words, do not use too much theological language your listener may be unfamiliar with—words like *justification, reconciliation,* and *sanctification.* If you do use such words, or if you use "Christian" expressions that are not everyday language (such as *born again*), be sure to clearly define what you mean by them.

- *Do not communicate in your testimony that true Christianity yields a bed of roses for believers.* Such a claim is simply not true. You might even share some of the struggles you have gone through since becoming a Christian. Your listener may identify with what you have gone through.

- *Do not be insensitive to the Mason's "works" background.* The apostle Paul in 1 Corinthians 2:14 stated: "A natural man does not accept the things of the Spirit of God, for they are foolishness to him; and he cannot understand them, because they are spiritually appraised" (NASB). The gospel of God's grace may not make much sense to a person who has been thoroughly schooled in the necessity of works— or ethics. For this reason, devote part of your testimony to how the gospel of God's grace set you free.

 As you finish your testimony, leave the Mason with a clear picture of how to become a Christian. Here are the most important points:

1. *God* desires *a personal relationship with human beings*

God created human beings (Genesis 1:27). And He did not just create them to exist all alone and apart from Him. He created them so that they might come into a personal relationship with Him. God had face-to-face encounters and fellowship with Adam and Eve, the first couple (Genesis 3:8-19). Just as God fellowshipped with them, so He desires to fellowship *with us* (1 John 1:5-7). God *loves* us (John 3:16).

   The problem is…

2. *Humanity has a sin problem that blocks a relationship with God*

When Adam and Eve chose to sin against God, they catapulted the entire human race—to which they gave birth—into sin. Since the time of Adam and Eve, every human being has been born into the world with a propensity to sin. The apostle Paul affirmed that "sin entered the world through one man, and death through sin" (Romans 5:12).

Jesus often spoke of sin in metaphors that illustrate the havoc it wreaks in one's life. He described sin as *blindness* (Matthew 23:16-26), *sickness* (Matthew 9:12), being *enslaved in bondage* (John 8:34), and *living in darkness* (John 8:12; 12:35-46). Moreover, Jesus taught that these are *universal conditions* and that all people are guilty before God (Luke 7:37-48).

Of course, some people are more morally upright than others. (The Mason to whom you are speaking may well be highly moral.) But even if we try to live a life of consistent good works, *we all fall short of God's infinite standards* (Romans 3:23). In a contest to see who can throw a rock to the moon, I am sure a muscular athlete would be able to throw the rock much farther than I could. But all humans fall far short of the task. Similarly, all of us fall short of measuring up to God's perfect holy standards.

Though the problem is a serious one, God has graciously provided a solution:

3. Jesus died for our sins and made salvation possible

God's absolute holiness demands that sin be punished. The good news of the gospel, however, is that Jesus has taken this punishment *entirely* on Himself. God loves us so much that He sent Jesus to bear the entire penalty for our sins!

It is critical that you help your Mason friend understand what Scripture says about this. Jesus affirmed that it was for the very purpose of dying that He came into the world (John 12:27). Moreover, He declared that His death was a sacrificial offering for the sins of humanity (Matthew 26:26-28). Jesus took His sacrificial mission with utmost seriousness, for He knew that without Him, humanity would certainly perish (Matthew 16:25; John 3:16) and spend eternity apart from God in a place of great suffering (Matthew 10:28; 11:23; 23:33; 25:41; Luke 16:22-28). Jesus therefore described His mission this way: "The

Son of Man did not come to be served, but to serve, and to give his life as a ransom for many" (Matthew 20:28).

4. Faith in Jesus is required

By His sacrificial death on the cross, Jesus took the sins of the entire world on Himself and made salvation available to everyone (1 John 2:2). But this salvation is not automatic. Only those who choose to believe in Christ are saved. This is the consistent testimony of the biblical Jesus. "For God so loved the world that he gave his one and only Son, that whoever *believes* in him shall not perish but have eternal life." "I am the resurrection and the life; he who *believes* in me will live even if he dies" (John 3:16; 11:25, emphasis added). Faith in Christ is what brings salvation, not obedience to the rules of the Masonic Lodge!

Choosing not to believe in Jesus, by contrast, leads to eternal condemnation: "Whoever believes in him is not condemned, but whoever *does not believe* stands condemned already because he has not believed in the name of God's one and only Son" (John 3:18, emphasis added).

5. We are free at last: forgiven of all sins

When a person believes in Christ the Savior, a wonderful thing happens. God forgives him of all his sins. *All of them!* He puts them completely out of His sight. Be sure to share the following verses, which speak of the forgiveness of those who have believed in Christ:

- "In him we have redemption through his blood, the forgiveness of sins, in accordance with the riches of God's grace" (Ephesians 1:7).

- "Their sins and lawless acts I will remember no more" (Hebrews 10:17).

- "Blessed is he whose transgressions are forgiven, whose sins are covered. Blessed is the man whose sin the Lord does not count against him and in whose spirit is no deceit" (Psalm 32:1,2).

- "As far as the east is from the west, so far has he removed our transgressions from us" (Psalm 103:12).

Such forgiveness is wonderful indeed, for—despite what the Masonic Lodge says—none of us can possibly work our way into salvation, or be good enough or ethical enough to warrant God's favor. Because of what Jesus has done for us, we freely receive the gift of salvation. It is a gift provided solely through the grace of God (Ephesians 2:8,9). And all of it is ours by simply believing in Jesus.

6. Don't put it off

Help your Mason friend see that it is a dangerous thing to put off turning to Christ for salvation, for no one knows the day of his or her death. What if it happens this evening? "Death is the destiny of every man; the living should take this to heart" (Ecclesiastes 7:2). "Seek the LORD while he may be found; call on him while he is near" (Isaiah 55:6).

7. Pray a simple prayer of faith

If the Mason to whom you are speaking expresses interest in trusting in *Jesus alone* for salvation (having understood the *true* scriptural teaching on Jesus and the gospel), lead him or her in a simple prayer like the one below. Be sure to emphasize that it is not the prayer itself that saves anyone. It is the *faith in one's heart* that brings salvation. The following prayer is just a simple expression of this:

Dear Jesus,
I want to have a relationship with You.
I know I can't save myself, because I'm a sinner.
Thank You for dying on the cross on my behalf.
I believe You died for me, and I accept Your free gift of salvation.
Thank You, Jesus. Amen.

8. *Welcome the Mason into God's forever family*

On the authority of the Word of God, you can now assure your Mason friend that he or she is a part of God's forever family. Encourage him or her with the prospect of spending all eternity by the side of Jesus in heaven!

For further information on witnessing to Masons, consult *Reasoning from the Scriptures with Masons*, pages 13–20, and 247–251.

An Exhortation: The Mason you've led to Christ still needs your help! Get him grounded in a good Bible-believing church. Introduce him to some of your Christian friends, and have your friends pray for him regularly. Realize that he may be carrying some psychological and spiritual "baggage" from his past association with the Masonic Lodge. Help him work through this. (It may be there is a Christian support group for former Masons in your area. If so, check this out as a possible support for your newly converted friend.)

Bibliography

Acker, J.W. *Strange Altars: A Scriptural Appraisal of the Lodge*. St. Louis: Concordia, 1959.

Allen, Raymond Lee. *Tennessee Craftsmen or Masonic Textbook*. Nashville, TN: Tennessee Board of Custodians Members, 1963.

Ankerberg, John, and John Weldon. *Cult Watch: What You Need to Know About Spiritual Deception*. Eugene, OR: Harvest House Publishers, 1991.

Ankerberg, John, and John Weldon. *Encyclopedia of Cults and New Religions*. Eugene, OR: Harvest House Publishers, 1999.

Ankerberg, John, and John Weldon. *The Secret Teachings of the Masonic Lodge*. Chicago: Moody Press, 1990.

Baigent, Michael, and Richard Leigh. *The Temple and the Lodge*. New York: Arcade, 1989.

Beliefs of Other Kinds: A Guide to Interfaith Witness in the United States. Atlanta, GA: Baptist Home Mission Board, 1984.

Blanchard, J. *Scottish Rite Masonry Illustrated (The Complete Ritual of the Ancient and Accepted Scottish Rite)*. Chicago: Charles T. Powner, 1979.

Boa, Kenneth. *Cults, World Religions, and You*. Wheaton, IL: Victor Books, 1979.

Bradley, Don. *Freemasonry in the 21ˢᵗ Century*. Burbank, CA: Native Planet Publishing, 1997.

Cerza, Alphonse. *Let There Be Light: A Study in Anti-Masonry*. Silver Spring, MD: The Masonic Service Association, 1983.

Coil, Henry Wilson. *A Comprehensive View of Freemasonry*. Richmond, VA: Macoy, 1973.

Enroth, Ronald. *A Guide to Cults and New Religions*. Downers Grove, IL: InterVarsity Press, 1983.

Enroth, Ronald. *The Lure of the Cults*. Downers Grove, IL: InterVarsity Press, 1987.

Gerstner, John H. *The Theology of the Major Sects*. Grand Rapids, MI: Baker Book House, 1980.

Gomes, Alan. *Unmasking the Cults*. Grand Rapids, MI: Zondervan Publishing House, 1995.

Hammond, William E. *What Masonry Means*. New York: Macoy Publishing, 1952.

Harris, Jack. *Freemasonry: The Invisible Cult in Our Midst*. Chattanooga, TN: Global, 1983.

Hoekema, Anthony A. *The Four Major Cults*. Grand Rapids, MI: Eerdmans, 1978.

Holy Bible (Temple Illustrated Edition). Nashville, TN: Holman, 1968.

Jones, Bernard E. *Freemason's Guide and Compendium*. London: Harrap, 1973.

Liturgy of the Ancient and Accepted Scottish Rite of Freemasonry for the Southern Jurisdiction of the United States. Washington, DC: The Supreme Council, 1982.

Martin, Walter. *Martin Speaks Out on the Cults*. Ventura, CA: Regal Books, 1983.

Martin, Walter. *The Kingdom of the Cults*. Minneapolis: Bethany House Publishers, 1999.

Martin, Walter. *The New Cults*. Ventura, CA: Regal Books, 1980.

Martin, Walter. *The Rise of the Cults*. Ventura, CA: Regal Books, 1983.

Mather, George A., and Larry A. Nichols. *Dictionary of Cults, Sects, Religions and the Occult*. Grand Rapids, MI: Zondervan Publishing House, 1993.

McDowell, Josh, and Don Stewart. *Understanding the Cults*. San Bernardino, CA: Here's Life Publishers, 1983.

McDowell, Josh, and Don Stewart. *Handbook of Today's Religions*. San Bernardino, CA: Here's Life Publishers, 1989.

Pike, Albert. *Morals and Dogma of the Ancient and Accepted Scottish Rite of Freemasonry*. Charleston, SC: The Supreme Council, 1906.

Robertson, Irvine. *What the Cults Believe*. Chicago: Moody Press, 1983.

Robinson, John J. *Born in Blood: The Lost Secrets of Freemasonry*. New York: M. Evans, 1989.

Rongstad, L. James. *The Lodge: How to Respond*. Saint Louis: CPH, 1995.

Swenson, Orville. *The Perilous Path of Cultism*. Caronport, Saskatchewan, Canada: Briercrest Books, 1987.

The Compact Guide to World Religions, ed. Dean C. Halverson. Minneapolis: Bethany House Publishers, 1996.

Thorn, Richard. *The Boy Who Cried Wolf: The Book that Breaks Masonic Silence*. New York: M. Evans and Company, 1994.

Tucker, Ruth. *Another Gospel: Alternative Religions and the New Age Movement*. Grand Rapids, MI: Zondervan Publishing House, 1989.

Voorhis, Harold V.B. *Facts for Freemasons*. Richmond, VA: Macoy Publishing and Masonic Supply Company, 1979.

Notes

Chapter 1—Masonry Is Not Just a Fraternal Organization—It Is a Religion

1. Henry Wilson Coil, *Coil's Masonic Encyclopedia* (New York: Macoy Publishing, 1961), p. 158.
2. Coil, p. 13.
3. Henry Wilson Coil, *A Comprehensive View of Freemasonry* (Richmond, VA: Macoy Publishing and Masonic Supply Company, 1973), p. 234.
4. Coil, *Coil's Masonic Encyclopedia,* p. 512.
5. Cited in L. James Rongstad, *The Lodge: How to Respond* (Saint Louis: CPH, 1995), p. 23.
6. Cited in Rongstad, p. 23.
7. *Liturgy of the Ancient and Accepted Scottish Rite of Freemasonry for the Southern Jurisdiction of the United States,* part 2 (Washington, DC: The Supreme Council, 1982), pp. 198-99.
8. Albert Pike, *Morals and Dogma* (Kila, Montana: Kessinger Publishing Company, n.d.), p. 219.
9. Pike, p. 219.
10. Albert Mackey, *Encyclopedia of Freemasonry* (Chicago: Masonic History, 1946), p. 619.
11. Mackey, p. 50.
12. See John J. Robinson, *Born in Blood: The Lost Secrets of Freemasonry* (New York: M. Evans and Company, 1989), p. 255.
13. Alphonse Cerza, *Let There Be Light: A Study In Anti-Masonry* (Silver Spring, MD: The Masonic Service Association, 1983), p. 41.
14. Richard Thorn, *The Boy Who Cried Wolf* (New York: M. Evans and Company, 1994), p. 83.
15. Robinson, p. 255.
16. Robinson, p. 256.
17. William E. Hammond, *What Masonry Means* (New York: Macoy Publishing, 1952), p. 99.
18. See Hammond, p. 15.
19. Thorn, p. 22.
20. *Liturgy of the Ancient and Accepted Scottish Rite of Freemasonry,* pp. 198-99.
21. Pike, p. 161.
22. Joseph Fort Newton, *The Religion of Masonry: An Interpretation* (Richmond, VA: Macoy, 1969), pp. 58-59.
23. Martin Wagner, *Freemasonry: An Interpretation* (Columbiana, OH: Missionary Service and Supply, n.d.), pp. 292-93.
24. Carl Claudy, *Foreign Countries: Our Gateway to the Interpretation and Development of Certain Symbols of Freemasonry* (Richmond, VA: Macoy Publishing, 1971), p. 23.
25. Mackey, p. 50.
26. As cited in George Mather and Larry Nichols, *Masonic Lodge* (Grand Rapids, MI: Zondervan, 1995), p. 31.
27. As cited in Mather and Nichols, p. 31.
28. Coil, *A Comprehensive View of Freemasonry,* p. 186.
29. John Ankerberg and John Weldon, *The Facts on the Masonic Lodge* (Eugene, OR: Harvest House Publishers, 1989), p. 20.
30. Mather and Nichols, p. 32.
31. Manly P. Hall, *The Lost Keys of Freemasonry* (Richmond, VA: Macoy Publishing, 1976), p. 33.
32. Mather and Nichols, pp. 34-35.

Chapter 2—Masonry Does Not Have Origins in Biblical Times

1. George Mather and Larry Nichols, *Masonic Lodge* (Grand Rapids: Zondervan, 1995), p. 7.
2. See John J. Robinson, *Born in Blood: The Lost Secrets of Freemasonry* (New York: M. Evans & Company, 1989), p. 178.
3. *Holy Bible: Deluxe Reference Edition* (Wichita, KS: Heirloom, 1988), p. 9.
4. Robinson, p. 177.
5. Robinson, p. 177.
6. J. Blanchard, *Scottish Rite Masonry Illustrated* (Chicago: Charles T. Powner, 1979), 2:290.
7. L. James Rongstad, *The Lodge: How to Respond* (Saint Louis: CPH, 1995), p. 12.

8. Harold V. B. Voorhis, *Facts for Freemasons* (Richmond, VA: Macoy Publishing and Masonic Supply Company, 1979), p. 17.
9. Robinson, p. xiii.
10. Michael Baigent and Richard Leigh, *The Temple and the Lodge* (New York: Arcade Publishing, 1989), p. 123.
11. See Baigent and Leigh, p. 126. See also William E. Hammond, *What Masonry Means* (New York: Macoy Publishing, 1952), p. 17ff; and Henry Wilson Coil, *A Comprehensive View of Freemasonry* (Richmond, VA: Macoy Publishing, 1973), p. 5.
12. Rongstad, p. 14.
13. Robert Morey, *The Origins and Teachings of Freemasonry* (Southbridge, MA: Crown Publications, 1990), p. 69.
14. Rongstad, p. 14.
15. John Ankerberg and John Weldon, *The Secret Teachings of the Masonic Lodge* (Chicago: Moody Press, 1990), p. 35.
16. Rongstad, p. 14.
17. Voorhis, p. 9.
18. Rongstad, p. 14.
19. Morey, p. 69.
20. See Ed Decker, *What You Need to Know About Masons* (Eugene, OR: Harvest House, 1992), p. 74.
21. Voorhis, p. 11.
22. Albert G. Mackey, *A Manual of the Lodge* (New York: Maynard, Merrill, & Co., 1898), p. 35.

Chapter 3—Masonic Rituals Are Highly Offensive
1. John J. Robinson, *Born in Blood* (New York: M. Evans & Company, 1989), p. 202.
2. Malcolm Duncan, *Duncan's Masonic Ritual and Monitor* (New York: David McKay, n.d.), p. 9.
3. Ron Carlson and Ed Decker, *Fast Facts on False Teachings* (Eugene: Harvest House, 1994), pp. 74-75.
4. William E. Hammond, *What Masonry Means* (New York: Macoy Publishing, 1952), p. 68.
5. Robinson, pp. 206-207.
6. Robinson, pp. 206-207.
7. Robinson, pp. 206-207.
8. George Mather and Larry Nichols, *Dictionary of Cults, Sects, Religions and the Occult* (Grand Rapids: Zondervan Publishing House, 1993), p. 11. See also Carlson and Decker, p. 75.
9. Robinson, p. 217.
10. Robinson, p. 207.
11. Robinson, pp. 207-208.
12. *Holy Bible: Deluxe Reference Edition* (Wichita, KS: Heirloom, 1988), p. 39.
13. *Adam Clarke's Commentary*, electronic database, 1996, Biblesoft.
14. Cited in Mather and Nichols, p. 11.
15. Walton Hannah, *Darkness Visible* (London: The Saint Austin Press, 1998), pp. 26-27.
16. Jim Tresner, "Conscience and the Craft," *Scottish Rite Journal* (February 1993):21.
17. John Ankerberg and John Weldon, *The Secret Teachings of the Masonic Lodge* (Chicago: Moody Press, 1990), p. 185.
18. Hannah, p. 21.
19. Robinson, p. 250.
20. Albert Mackey, *A Manual of the Lodge* (New York: Maynard, Merrill, & Co., 1898), p. 41.

Chapter 4—The Bible Is Not Just One of Many Holy Books—It Is Uniquely God's Word
1. Vindex, *Light Invisible* (Boston: Masonic Publishers, 1996), p. 40.
2. Henry Wilson Coil, *Coil's Masonic Encyclopedia* (New York: Macoy Publishing, 1961), p. 520.
3. Albert G. Mackey, *A Manual of the Lodge* (New York: Maynard, Merrill, & Co., 1898), p. 30.
4. Albert Pike, *Morals and Dogma* (Charleston, SC: The Supreme Council, 1906), pp. 744-45.
5. Richard Thorn, *The Boy Who Cried Wolf* (New York: M. Evans and Company, 1994), p. 70.
6. Norman Geisler and William Nix, *A General Introduction to the Bible* (Chicago: Moody Press, 1978), p. 28.
7. Donald J. Wiseman, "Archaeological Confirmation of the Old Testament"; in Norman L. Geisler, *Christian Apologetics* (Grand Rapids: Baker Book House, 1976), p. 322.
8. William F. Albright; cited in Josh McDowell, *Evidence that Demands a Verdict* (San Bernardino, CA: Campus Crusade for Christ, 1972), p. 68.
9. Douglas Groothuis, *Confronting the New Age* (Downers Grove, IL: InterVarsity, 1988), p. 85.

Chapter 5— The World Religions Do Not All Worship the Same God

1. Jim Tresner; cited in George Mather and Larry Nichols, *Masonic Lodge* (Grand Rapids: Zondervan, 1995), p. 41.
2. William E. Hammond, *What Masonry Means* (New York: Macoy, 1952), p. 159.
3. Albert Mackey, *Encyclopedia of Freemasonry* (New York: Masonic History Co., 1920), p. 48.
4. Mackey, p. 48.
5. Henry Wilson Coil, *A Comprehensive View of Freemasonry* (Richmond, VA: Macoy, 1973), p. 192.
6. Albert Mackey, *Revised Encyclopedia of Freemasonry* (Richmond, VA: Macoy, 1966), 1:409-10.
7. J.W. Acker, *Strange Altars* (St. Louis: Concordia, 1959), p. 37.
8. Henry Wilson Coil, *Coil's Masonic Encyclopedia* (New York: Macoy, 1961), p. 516.
9. Martin Wagner, *Freemasonry: An Interpretation* (Columbiana, OH: Missionary Service and Supply, n.d.), pp. 338-39.
10. Lewis M. Hopfe, *Religions of the World* (New York: Macmillan, 1991), p. 98.
11. Walter Martin, *The New Cults* (Ventura: Regal Books, 1980), p. 82.
12. J. Isamu Yamamoto, *Hinduism, TM & Hare Krishna* (Grand Rapids, MI: Zondervan, 1997), p. 11.
13. Dean Halverson, *The Compact Guide to World Religions* (Minneapolis: Bethany, 1996), p. 89.
14. Yamamoto, p. 11.
15. Hopfe, p. 99.
16. Mark Albrecht, "Hinduism," in *Evangelizing the Cults* (Ann Arbor, MI: Servant, 1990), p. 22.
17. See Ron Rhodes, *Islam: What You Need to Know* (Eugene: Harvest House Publishers, 2000).
18. Cited in Walton Hannah, *Darkness Visible* (London: The Saint Austin Press, 1998), p. 35.
19. Hannah, p. 34.
20. Hannah, p. 42.

Chapter 6—Jesus Is Not Just a Good Moral Teacher—He Is Uniquely the Son of God

1. There are some Masonic Lodges that acknowledge Jesus, but they are fewer in number than those that do not.
2. Jack Harris, *Freemasonry: The Invisible Cult in Our Midst* (Chattanooga, TN: Global, 1983), p. 112.
3. *Encyclopedia of Freemasonry*, vol. 1, p. 149.
4. Albert Pike, *Morals and Dogma* (Kila, Montana: Kessinger Publishing Company, n.d.), p. 540.
5. Pike, p. 308.
6. Richard Thorn, *The Boy Who Cried Wolf* (New York: M. Evans and Company, 1994), p. 25.
7. C.S. Lewis, *Mere Christianity* (New York: Macmillan, 1960), pp. 40-41.
8. Robert L. Reymond, *Jesus, Divine Messiah: The Old Testament Witness* (Fearn, Ross-Shire, Scotland: Christian Focus Publications, 1990), pp. 78-84.
9. See George Mather and Larry Nichols, *Dictionary of Cults, Sects, Religions and the Occult* (Grand Rapids: Zondervan Publishing House, 1993), p. 119.
10. Yogi, *Meditations of Maharishi Mahesh Yogi*, 123-24; cited in J. Isamu Yamamoto, *Hinduism, TM & Hare Krishna* (Grand Rapids: Zondervan, 1996), p. 48.

Chapter 7—Salvation Is Not By Ethical Living—It Is by Faith in Christ

1. H.L. Haywood, *The Great Teachings of Masonry* (Richmond, VA: Macoy, 1971), pp. 138-39.
2. L. James Rongstad, *The Lodge: How to Respond* (Saint Louis: CPH, 1995), p. 22.
3. Grand Lodge of Texas, *Monitor of the Lodge* (Grand Lodge of Texas, 1982), p. 19.
4. Jack Harris, *Freemasonry: The Invisible Cult in Our Midst* (Chattanooga, TN: Global, 1983), p. 132.
5. *Mackey's Revised Encyclopedia of Freemasonry*, 1:269.
6. Rongstad, *The Lodge*, p. 47.
7. Albert G. Mackey, *A Manual of the Lodge* (New York: Maynard, Merrill, & Co., 1898), p. 16.
8. E.K. Simpson and F.F. Bruce, *Commentary on the Epistles to the Ephesians and Colossians* (Grand Rapids: Eerdmans, 1975), p. 50.
9. John Ankerberg and John Weldon, *The Secret Teachings of the Masonic Lodge* (Chicago: Moody Press, 1990), p. 142.
10. Martin Luther; cited in J.I. Packer, *Knowing Christianity* (Wheaton, IL: Harold Shaw Publishers, 1995), p. 94.
11. *The Bible Knowledge Commentary*, New Testament, eds. John F. Walvoord and Roy B. Zuck (Wheaton, IL: Victor Books, 1989), p. 825.

Chapter 8—Masonry Is Connected to Occultism and Paganism

1. H.L. Haywood, *Great Teachings of Masonry* (Kingsport, TN: Southern Publishers, 1923), p. 94.

2. See John Ankerberg and John Weldon, *The Secret Teachings of the Masonic Lodge* (Chicago: Moody Press, 1990), pp. 216-18.
3. Cited in E.M. Storms, *Should a Christian Be a Mason?* (Kirkwood, MO: Impact, 1999), p. 20.
4. Vindex, *Light Invisible* (Boston: Masonic Publishers, 1996), p. 11.
5. As cited in Ankerberg and Weldon, p. 219.
6. Ankerberg and Weldon, p. 219.
7. Albert Mackey, *Revised Encyclopedia of Freemasonry* (Richmond, VA: Macoy, 1966), p. 375.
8. Ankerberg and Weldon, p. 215.
9. Albert Mackey, *An Encyclopedia of Freemasonry* (New York: Masonic History Co., 1920), pp. 233, 364-65, 587.
10. See Albert Pike, *Morals and Dogma* (Kila, Montana: Kessinger, n.d.), pp. 255, 290-91, 364-65, 376.
11. See Pike, p. 255.
12. Pike, p. 460.
13. Pike, pp. 22, 23.
14. Vindex, p. 9.
15. L. James Rongstad, *The Lodge: How to Respond* (Saint Louis: CPH, 1995), p. 12.
16. Martin Wagner, *Freemasonry: An Interpretation* (Columbiana, OH: Missionary Service and Supply, n.d.), p. 253.
17. Ankerberg and Weldon, p. 253.
18. Ankerberg and Weldon, p. 249.
19. Charles C. Ryrie, *A Survey of Bible Doctrine* (Chicago: Moody Press, 1980), p. 94.
20. Charles C. Ryrie, *Balancing the Christian Life* (Chicago: Moody Press, 1990), p. 124.
21. John Davis, *Moses and the Gods of Egypt* (Grand Rapids: Baker, 1986), p. 97.
22. Norman Geisler, *A Popular Survey of the Old Testament* (Grand Rapids: Baker, 1977), p. 56.
23. Davis, p. 108.

Chapter 9—Christians Should Not Participate in Freemasonry

1. "Freemasonry Report," prepared by David W. Atchison, Executive Committee, Southern Baptist Convention, June 15-17, 1993.
2. "Freemasonry Report."
3. "Freemasonry Report."
4. Eddy D. Field II and Eddy D. Field III, "Freemasonry and the Christian," *The Master's Seminary Journal,* (Fall 1994): 141-57.
5. Ron Carlson and Ed Decker, *Fast Facts on False Teachings* (Eugene, OR: Harvest House Publishers, 1994), pp. 74-75.
6. John J. Robinson, *Born in Blood: The Lost Secrets of Freemasonry* (New York: M. Evans & Company, 1989), pp. 206-207.
7. Robinson, p. 255.
8. Henry Wilson Coil, *A Comprehensive View of Freemasonry* (Richmond, VA: Macoy, 1973), p. 192.
9. See, for example, Albert Pike, *Morals and Dogma of the Ancient and Accepted Scottish Rite of Freemasonry* (Kila, Montana: Kessinger Publishing Company, n.d.), p. 255.
10. George Mather and Larry Nichols, *Masonic Lodge* (Grand Rapids, MI: Zondervan, 1995), p. 26.
11. Walton Hannah, *Darkness Visible* (London: The Saint Austin Press, 1998), pp. 18-19.
12. Hannah, p. 39.
13. Field and Field, pp. 141-57.
14. Cited in Arthur Pruess, *Dictionary of Secret and Other Societies* (St. Louis: B. Herder Company, 1924), p. 143.

Chapter 10—Jesus Has Changed My Life Forever

1. *Draper's Book of Quotations for the Christian World* (Grand Rapids: Baker, 1992), p. 73.
2. *Draper's Book of Quotations,* p. 65.
3. John Blanchard, *More Gathered Gold* (Darlington, Durham, Gr. Britain: Evangelical Press, 1986).
4. *Draper's Book of Quotations,* p. 66.
5. *Draper's Book of Quotations,* p. 66.
6. Blanchard.
7. Blanchard.
8. Walter Martin, "The Do's and Don'ts of Witnessing to Cultists," *Christian Research Newsletter,* January-February 1992, p. 4.